HOOKED
LEARNING TO FISH

BY AL BROWN
ILLUSTRATED BY HOPE MCCONNELL

First published in 2025

Text © Al Brown, 2025

Illustrations © Hope McConnell, 2025, unless credited below

All rights reserved. No part of this book may be reproduced or transmitted in any form or by any means, electronic or mechanical, including photocopying, recording or by any information storage and retrieval system, without prior permission in writing from the publisher.

Allen & Unwin Aotearoa New Zealand
Level 2, 10 College Hill, Freemans Bay
Auckland 1011, New Zealand
+64 (9) 377 3800
auckland@allenandunwin.com
www.allenandunwin.co.nz

83 Alexander Street
Crows Nest NSW 2065, Australia
+61 (2) 8425 0100

EU Authorised Representative: Easy Access System Europe, Mustamäe tee 50, 10621 Tallinn, Estonia, gpsr.requests@easproject.com

A catalogue record for this book is available from the National Library of New Zealand.

ISBN 978 1 991142 16 0

Design by Gary Stewart, The Gas Project
Set in Futura, Farson, Courier and Pleasurize
Illustrations on endpapers and pages 28–9 © Fishserve, reproduction by Hope McConnell
Printed in China by 1010 Printing Limited

10 9 8 7 6 5 4 3 2 1

TO 'MATTO' . . . THANKS FOR SHARING YOUR EXTRAORDINARY KNOWLEDGE, HILARITY, DUBIOUS STORIES AND CONSTANT COMMENTARY, WHETHER RIVERSIDE OR ON THE BIG BLUE.

HE KARAKIA MŌ TE HĪ IKA
TRADITIONAL FISHING KARAKIA

Kuku, kuku ika, kuku wehiwehi,
Takina ko koe nā, te iho o ika,
Te iho o Tangaroa —
Uara ki uta rā, uara ki tai rā.

Hold tight, hold the fish, hold tight with fearsome power,
You are led along, the essence of the fish,
The essence of Tangaroa —
Desired on the land, desired on the sea.

This karakia is said to Tangaroa, god of the sea, asking for bountiful fishing. The written record of this karakia is attributed to Mohi Ruatapu, of Tokomaru Bay, a great Ngāti Porou tohunga, who in his later years recorded the stories and songs of his iwi.

CONTENTS

INTRODUCTION	6
TE HĪ IKA — MĀORI FISHING	16
SUSTAINABILITY	22
LEARNING THE LINGO	32
YOUR LUCKY FISHING HAT	40
FISHING KIT	44
KNOTS AND NOTS	68
SAFETY IS NO ACCIDENT	76
FISHING FROM A WHARF	80
FISHING FROM A SMALL BOAT OR KAYAK	86
SURFCASTING	92
ON THE FLY	98
YOU'VE CAUGHT A FISH! NOW WHAT?	110
COOKING UP YOUR CATCH	118
INDEX	142
ABOUT THE AUTHOR	144

INTRODUCTION

Catching your first fish is a super-special moment. It will be a treasured occasion that will be etched into your memory for the rest of your life.

It will also be special for the lucky person that has taken you for your first fishing adventure, as they will get a huge buzz witnessing your excitement and relive the moment that they caught their own first fish.

Learning to fish is so much fun, and is likely to be the start of an exciting lifelong journey. The learning never really ends as you continually build your knowledge through each thrilling fishing experience.

You are going to love learning how to tie knots, bait up a hook and cast a lure. Some skills are easy to master, others will take more time and practice. Each new technique and experience will build on what you have already learnt, and as your repertoire grows so will your confidence and expertise. However, I've got to tell you that once you start you are going to struggle to stop — there is just too much fun to be had when there is a fishing tackle involved!

Another big bonus? With all the practical skills you learn when you start your fishing odyssey, there are a bunch of other lessons that will serve you well in general life. Words like determination, perseverance and patience play a big part in fishing, as they do in day-to-day trials and tribulations.

Fishing is of course an outdoor endeavour. You will find yourself in some pretty awesome locations, which plays a big part in the enjoyment of fishing.

'You can't buy happiness, but you can go fishing.' — Anonymous

While just being present in these stunning environments is good for the soul, it is also an important aspect in becoming a competent angler. Experience comes from being in tune, staying curious, learning through observation and understanding the unique settings you will find yourself in.

I find fishing a great way to clear my head — there is something almost spiritual about being around water. Sometimes it's the vastness, other times the stillness, the deepness or the speed of the flowing water. You will also find yourself having fun in many locations, be it a lake, river, stream, lagoon, estuary or the ocean. Each fishing adventure will be different from the last. You'll find something new and interesting about each scenario, whether it's fishing for sprats and herrings off a wharf next to a thousand-tonne container ship, wandering up an urban stream with a fly rod on the outskirts of town, or simply dropping a baited hook or two from a boat on the 'big blue'.

This is the thing about learning to fish: you will find that it constantly challenges your thoughts . . . Am I in the right spot? What if I change my lure? What is the tide doing? Should I change my bait? The size of my hook? The weight of my sinker? Dang . . . you'll even consider the way you hold your tongue!

Recreational fishing is incredibly popular around the world. Wherever you go, if you meet people who fish you will be immediately connected by your shared passion for hunting fish.

Whether talking about past adventures, or sharing tips or local knowledge, there is a universal camaraderie that comes with being part of the same club worldwide, no matter where you are from.

The wonderful and incredibly lucky thing about fishing in New Zealand is you are never far from water that fish inhabit, even in the towns and cities. An example: I have stood under the Auckland Harbour Bridge along with a bunch of perfect strangers just metres apart, fishing for squid in the dead of night as the cars and trucks rumbled overhead. Unique for sure, and serious fun!

While I often fish alone, like most things, it's often more of a good time when you are with a couple of mates who can share in the adventure that you are all experiencing. Fishing is an activity that truly bonds and creates enduring friendships. There will always be plenty of competitiveness, a good deal of sledging and banter, but there is also a ton of pleasure that comes with witnessing good buddies catching a fish.

It's only natural that everyone wants to catch the biggest fish — especially when fishing with your mates. However, there can only be one winner on the day, so while there can be a certain amount of smugness when you come out on top, my advice to you is that gloating should always be kept in check! Tomorrow is another day, in another spot, with another bait and fingers crossed another good outcome, but you never know who will get the glory of snaffling the largest catch of the day.

To my budding new anglers, I trust this book inspires you all to learn the wonderful pursuit of how to catch fish. Something that dawned on me when I was putting this all together was that we fishers never really stop learning. And while I have been fishing for as long as I can remember, there is hardly a day when I'm out there doing it that I'm not discovering something new. So what started out as a simple 'how to fish' book has now morphed into something that I trust appeals to all those who, from time to time, like to wet a line. Part reference, part how-to, part tongue in cheek, part conversation, part recipes, part education, part nostalgia . . . and, of course, the most important part of all is having ridiculous amounts of fun.

A LOVE OF FISHING

While I struggle to recollect many of the special moments from when I was a wee lad growing up, there are some enduring memories that I vividly recall from that period of my life. Weirdly, they all had the same three things in common: a hook, a line and a sinker!

I grew up on a farm in the central Wairarapa region. With no ocean or lake within cooee, my only fishing option was down at what I used to call 'the river'. It was more like a windy willow-lined muddy creek with the odd deep hole here and there, but there were also a few spots that you could easily step across with gumboots on.

My eeling line was rough brown hessian twine, about 5 to 10 metres in length, simply wound around a quarter inch-thick stick or a piece of kindling. The hooks were pretty basic, long shank if I recall, and the sinker was usually one or two rusted old nuts. As the creek had a minimal amount of current, I only needed just enough weight to hold the baited hook in position.

Bait was whatever I could find. It was always a protein of some sort — from raw sheep's liver or kidneys, leftover cooked meat from a roast or even some luncheon sausage if things were desperate. My bait of choice, though, was a piece of raw mutton containing a little fat, usually sourced from a carcass hanging in the shed where we butchered sheep for the shepherds and their families.

Burley (see page 35) was a bit of a luxury and usually a hit or miss affair. We would use roadkill, such as a freshly skinned possum or rabbit, bound with some old bailing twine and then tied to a low-hanging willow branch or a stick driven into the mud bank.

Another highly prized eel attractant was rotten eggs that we occasionally found near or around the chook house in odd spots outside their hatch. Breaking them directly into the water a few metres above where I was eeling, while super stinky, was very efficient in attracting the attention of the slithery black 'snakes'.

If I close my eyes, I can still easily visualise and experience the thrill and elation of seeing a dark serpent-like shape appear from the shadows under the bank, gliding effortlessly up the current, nostrils flared, coming close to my bait. Staying as still as possible, I would fix my eyes on the hessian line where it entered the water. Seeing the line begin to move was always a heart-racing thrill. Gripping the line tightly and ever so slowly lifting it, and feeling the weight come on with the first head shake as the eel realises it has a hook in its mouth . . . that feeling never gets old.

When I was a kid, hardly a week would go by without at least one eeling mission. The 'river' meandered for miles in both directions, so finding new spots to eel was always an adventure on a push bike. On the odd occasion that I had a mate staying over, we would often go eeling at night. We would light a fire on the edge of the river and eel into the night, as they were attracted to the light. We would always let the eels go — unless it happened to be shearing time on the farm, which gave me the opportunity to trade the eels with the shearers for large bottles of fizzy. The travelling shearing gangs often stayed on the farms, and with a constant diet of sheep meat the eels were always appreciated.

The next vivid memory I recall from when I was young is of trolling for kahawai out of our little tinny with its smoky old seagull engine. While I loved eeling, fishing in a saltwater situation was in a different stratosphere altogether. We were trolling between Kapiti Island and the mainland, and caught two or three kahawai that day. I'm pretty sure that would have been the first time I held an actual fishing rod with a reel attached.

Pound for pound, kahawai is one of the hardest fighting and most exciting fish to catch. We are blessed to have such a wonderful species inhabiting most coastal areas around Aotearoa. They are battlers and you can always guarantee they will give you a good scrap — they cavort and often jump clear out of the water in an attempt to dislodge those classic heavy-metal lures armed with deadly sharp treble hooks that many will be familiar with.

That was a super high-octane fishing experience, and one which I believe lit the spark for a lifetime of chasing aquatic dreams. I still regularly fish for kahawai with a fly rod — off the boat and from the shore. My brother Jeremy even targets (and catches) the mighty kingfish on a fly rod, which is an extraordinary feat.

From those early days to my sixtieth year, I have tried all sorts of fishing styles and disciplines, and have targeted all manner of fish species here and overseas. I guess like many recreational sports there is a certain tendency to get obsessive! And while a lucky few will be fortunate enough to grapple and engage in several recreational outdoor activities, many choose to become a purist in their chosen discipline, dedicating much personal recreational time to mastering their pursuit.

In fishing, there is a term often bandied about. It's called the 10 percent club. It goes something like this: 10 percent of the people who fish recreationally catch 90 percent of the fish. Unfortunately, that means that 90 percent of the people only catch 10 percent of the fish. I think there's some truth to this. Even though I'm constantly working on my fishing skills, I don't think I'm in that top 10 percent . . . yet! There is only one way to become a member of that hallowed and revered club, and that is to commit to complete dedication to the sport. Which essentially means reading, watching, talking about, learning, trialling, experimenting, observing, proving, testing and constantly questioning everything in the fishing space.

Let's not forget, these esteemed members of the 10 percent club will have also endured a huge amount of heartache, despair and grief along the way. For while their phones all contain hundreds of fish they have landed, it is the ones that got away that will continue to haunt and torment them for the rest of their years. What I love about that is that even if they could, those anglers wouldn't change a thing, and they will have cherished each and every minute of their fishing journey to date. It is their single-minded, dogged commitment and determination to master the art of fishing that I admire most.

I love all types of fishing. I fish out of boats, kayaks, off the rocks. I'm mad about walking up rivers with a fly rod, surfcasting off sandy beaches and catching squid in the dead of the night.

It can be as simple as fishing for sprats with a child off a wharf, to chasing the elusive bone fish in the clear lagoons of Rarotonga. (I've caught only one, after many hours of trying!)

While I do get more of a kick out of certain fishing opportunities than others, they all give me a thrill one way or another. It all revolves around the anticipation of the adventure ahead. Anticipation of the unknown, the unexpected and the expected.

The one thing (besides a little luck) that I have learnt over the years about fishing, which applies to any of the angling disciplines, is that it's about the 'three rights'. Being in the right location at the right time with the right gear.
Good luck out there!

TE HĪ IKA — MĀORI FISHING

In the past, now and into the future the ocean will always mean so much more than just a food source. It is a sacred place of spiritual significance and cultural knowledge, as well as traditional fishing skills which have been passed down the generations and are still in use today.

EARLY MĀORI FISHING PRACTICES

For Māori who lived on the coast, the ocean filled their kete kai with all the extraordinary treasures living there. They were expert and ingenious fishers, always respecting and honouring Tangaroa, god of the sea.

Māori naturally understood the importance of sustainability within their fishing endeavours. Their instinctive and deep-rooted connection with nature and the environment was as indisputable as it was significant.

Through observing nature, experts within the individual tribes understood the signs for successful fishing. They used the maramataka, the Māori lunar calendar, to decide when and where to harvest their kai. They understood the movements, breeding cycles and seasons for numerous fish species.

Much of the equipment they used to fish originally came from Polynesia but worked equally well here in Aotearoa.

Fishing nets were made from green flax. There were small hand-held individual nets and massive seine-style nets that could be close to a kilometre in length. Dried-out gourds or light driftwood were used as floats, while stones were attached to the bottom to keep the net spread apart.

Individual fishing lines were made of flax strands that had been twisted together and were very strong. Hooks were skilfully carved out of wood, bone, stones and shells. Not only were they great for catching fish, but they are also absolute works of art.

One ingenious method used a thing called a gorge. It was a sharp piece of bone that would be disguised inside a piece of bait, and when the fish swallowed it, the tension on the line caused it to jam in the throat of the fish, which was then successfully landed. Pāua and mother-of-pearl shells were used to make lures to attract fish such as kahawai, araara (trevally) and the like.

Pātiki (flounder) were particularly prized. These fish were caught in estuaries and harbours using sharp barbed spears.

Crayfish pots were constructed using young vines or branches that were bent into shape, secured with strong and versatile flax threads.

Fishing grounds were fiercely guarded by individual tribes, and were located by lining up various points and landmarks from the shore.

Many rituals, routines and protocols were handed down from the ancestors. Karakia were always offered to Tangaroa before venturing out, as a sign of respect and an appeal to the god of the sea to bless them with a bountiful catch, keep them out of danger and safeguard their return unscathed to the shore. Karakia were also recited on the return from a fishing trip as a way of giving thanks to Tangaroa.

Other rituals included putting back the first landed fish to pay respect to Tangaroa, a practice still common today. The first fish is called 'te ika whakataki'.

Certain waters were regulated by customary law and practices, such as limiting certain species to being caught at particular times of the year. Fishing grounds were also monitored and sometimes were closed in the form of a rāhui. These actions were all taken in the name of conservation, protecting both the fish and the fishing grounds.

Harvested fish were never scaled and gutted near or on the fishing grounds. This task was always performed well away and above the high-tide mark. Cooked food was never to be in contact with the ocean, as this was believed to contaminate the fishing grounds.

None of the catch was wasted. Fish were steamed in a hāngī, or dried out in the sun then stored in pātaka (raised store huts) to be eaten later.

Often the catch, along with dried fish, edible dried seaweed and shark oil, was gifted to inland tribes or exchanged for other food such as preserved birds.

When Captain James Cook visited the Marlborough Sounds in 1773 and compared Māori fishing skills with those on his ship, he wrote: 'We were by no means such expert fishers as them, nor were any of our methods of fishing equal to theirs.'

MĀORI FISHING TERMS

aho	fishing line
hīnaki	eel trap
kupenga	fishing net
matau	fish hook
matira	fishing rod
moana	ocean
pā	weir to trap eels
pehu	spear
tāruke	crayfish pot

MĀORI FISHING LEGENDS

Māori culture has long embraced myths and legends around fishing and the ocean — many of these stories are used to teach the values of caring for the ocean and the kai moana (food from the sea). Do you know these Māori legends?

Tangaroa, God of the Sea, and Ikatere, God of the Fishes

In Māori mythology, Tangaroa is the god of the sea. He was one of the children of Ranginui (the sky father) and Papatūānuku (the earth mother).

Tangaroa had a son, Punga, who in turn was the father of Ikatere and Tūtewehiwehi.

When Tangaroa's brother Tāwhirimātea, the god of wind and storms, went to war against his brothers for separating Ranginui and Papatūānuku (and letting light into the world), legend says that Ikatere and Tūtewehiwehi fled for their lives.

Ikatere went to the sea where he and his children became fish, while Tūtewehiwehi ventured inland and he and his offspring became reptiles.

Māui and the giant fish

Another well-known legend is the story of a demi-god called Māui. It is said that Māui hooked up the North Island of Aotearoa using the jawbone of his ancestor Murirangawhenua as a hook.

Māui had wanted to go fishing with his brothers, but they said no. So he stowed away in his brothers' waka and emerged when they were far from shore. As Māui fished, he chanted a karakia and soon he hooked an enormous fish. As he pulled the fish to the surface, Māui's brothers were scared they would drown, and begged him to cut the line. Māui held on, and fished up the land that we know as Te Ika-a-Māui (Māui's great fish) — the North Island.

As Māui's brothers argued over which pieces of the giant fish they would claim, they hacked at the land. Their cuts formed the mountains and valleys throughout the North Island.

The North Island itself is in the shape of a stingray (whai). North Cape is known as Te Hiku-o-te-Ika (the tail of the stingray) and Wellington is known as Te-Upoko-o-te-Ika (the head of the stingray).

SUSTAINABILITY

Sustainability is a word you hear a lot about these days — it's sometimes used so much in so many different ways that it loses its meaning.

What does it actually mean? Let's break it down:

Sustain: to support or keep something going

Ability: the power or skill to do something

So fishing sustainably is all about fishing in a way that leaves enough fish to keep their species going strong for generations to come. If we don't fish sustainably, eventually there'll be nothing left to catch!

So, let's talk about a few things to keep front of mind when going fishing.

CATCH AND RELEASE

The phrase 'catch and release' has been bandied around for quite some time now. It became a term when passionate anglers targeting large trout in back-country streams realised that if you 'donked' the only fish in the pool on the head post-battle, it would take quite some time for that fish to be replaced by another beautiful big trout.

They also understood that if a carefully released trout was put back into the stream alive and well, there was every chance that when they returned to that same pool in the same stream in the future, they could try and fool it again . . . and again, and again. Many fly-fishermen will be able to recall catching the same fish in the same spot on many different occasions.

Here's the thing: while the trout may get a bit sick of the occasional skirmish ending with a little sting in their lip, the alternatives on offer are relatively dire. Either hanging on the wall gathering dust or ending up on a platter, covered in Béarnaise sauce!

Joking aside, the term 'catch and release' is becoming more and more mainstream in most fishing circles. And while there will most likely always be a bunch of short-sighted fishers out there who want to kill everything they hook, there is definitely a new and very passionate wave of seasoned fishers spreading the gospel on better fishing practices. Most of it is based around sustainability, common sense and understanding that this fishing lark that we get so much pleasure from is ultimately finite, and we all must play our part in ensuring that future generations get to enjoy and experience all the fun we caring anglers currently do.

While it may seem counterintuitive to many, once you start releasing fish, you begin to see fishing in a whole new light. You immediately have an appreciation and understanding of how precious and vulnerable fish are. When you adhere to some very simple practices around how to handle fish removed from the water, there is a massive pleasure garnered from seeing the fish back in its environment, often giving a flick of its tail as if to say thanks as it heads down through the water column.

We all have cameras and most of us enjoy a little 'show and tell' so you needn't miss out on the 'brag shot', but there is so much good that comes with the thought that the beautiful specimen of a fish that you are showing off is still likely to be out there somewhere, alive and well.

Here are some of the best catch and release practices:

- Fish with barbless or circle hooks.
- Have a wet towel to handle the fish and to use when removing the hook.
- A wet rag over the head of the fish will also help calm it.
- Release the fish back into the water as quickly as possible.
- When releasing, cradle the fish from its underside, allowing the water to move through its gills while acclimatising it back into its environment.

You will know instinctively when the fish is ready to swim away. Release it and enjoy the moment.

CATCHING A RANGE OF SPECIES

It's really easy to fall into the habit of just cooking one or two species of fish that you're familiar with. If you live near the top of the North Island, people tend to target snapper or kingfish; in the middle of the country it's tarakihi and hāpuka; and in the south it's blue cod or one of the plentiful flat-fish like flounder or sole.

These fish are delicious, no doubt, but there are many other species that are just as wonderful to eat. When popular varieties get overfished, their numbers decline. So don't ignore the other plentiful species, including the small fish like sprats, piper, herring and mackerel, as excellent species to eat.

The first question to ask yourself when you head out for a day of fishing is how much fish do I need? The daily catch limit is not a target. Keeping just a few fish to eat doesn't stop you from having a great day's fishing — you can put any fish that you're not going to eat back in the briny. It is a wonderful feeling to watch a fish swimming away to fight another day.

All fish are precious — handle the live ones with care as you release them, and handle the dead ones with respect, eating as much of the fish as you can.

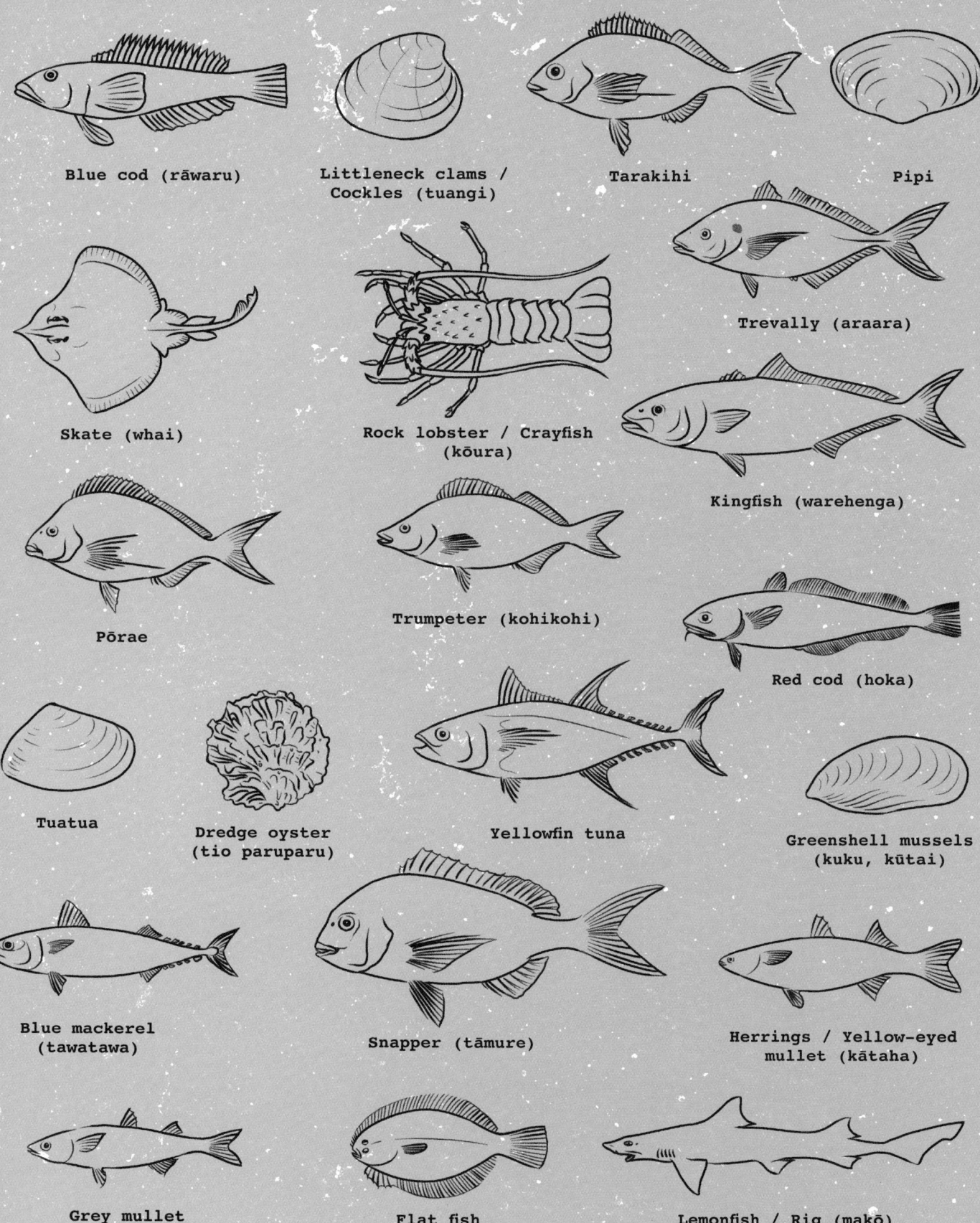

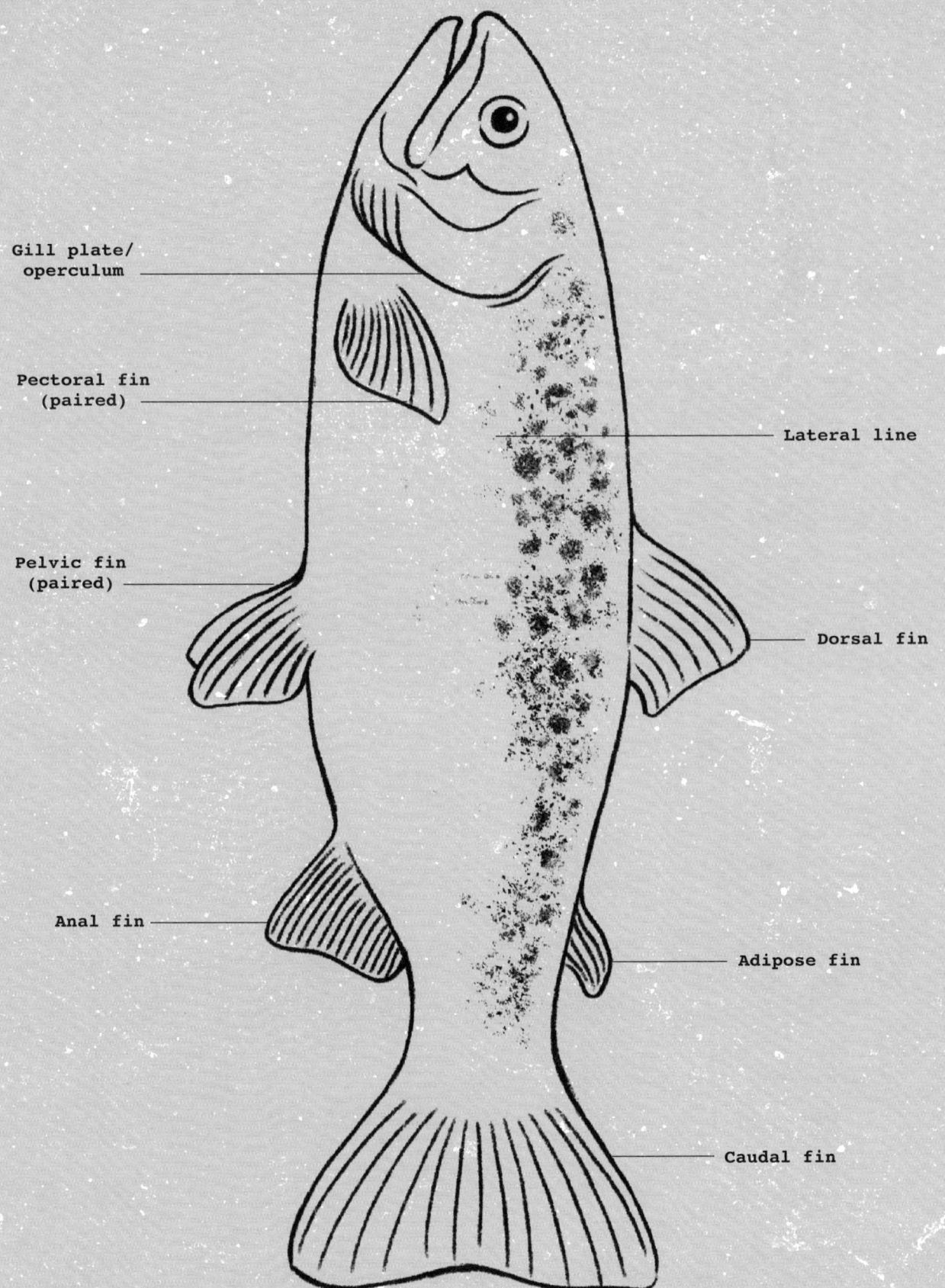

USING ALL OF THE FISH

When you catch, prepare, cook and eat the bounty of your adventures, you're honouring the fish that you've caught.

There's plenty more of the fish to use than just two perfect fish fillets. I recommend scaling the fish first — it's much easier to fillet that way — and then cooking the fillets with the skin on. There's a tiny layer of fat between the skin and the fillet which has a beautiful flavour. The skin will crisp up and give you a texture like crackling.

After you've discarded the innards and removed the fillets from your fish, you'll be left with what is essentially the throat of the fish, which includes some of the belly, the gill plate and the pectoral fin. Remove the throat then slice down the middle to give two 'wings', which are delicious to eat. And the remainder — the head and bones — can be used to make fish stock, which you can turn into a tasty chowder.

If you're preparing a large fish, there are two more things you can do with its frame: scrape away any flesh still attached to the bone with a spoon to make lovely ceviche; or chop the frame into manageable pieces then smoke or roast them for a great snack.

Another sustainable way to prepare your fish is to gut it and then cook it whole, especially if it's a flat-fish like flounder. You can barbecue, roast or steam it with spectacular results. Yes there'll be bones to deal with, but I like that it slows you down, making time at the table to really enjoy the food. Once you've eaten the top side of the fish, you can peel out the spine and skeleton, leaving the underside with far fewer bones to deal with.

'The two best times to fish are when it's rainin', and when it ain't.'
— Patrick McManus

LEARNING THE LINGO

Fishing has its own special language, full of slang and jargon as well as specialised terms for the technical stuff. Like any language it keeps changing, with new words and expressions added all the time.

Part of fishing is being a good storyteller — so pepper your yarns with a few of these words and it'll seem like you know what you're talking about!

DESCRIBING YOUR CATCH

Large fish (to be used regularly): monster, stonker, lunker, donkey, hog, horse, whopper.

Small fish (to be used as little as possible): tiddler, sprat, shrimp, small fry, dink, minnow.

FISHING TERMS

Backing: the rearmost section of a fishing line that is connected to the spool of the fishing reel. It bulks up the reel and is connected to the mainline.

Bag limit: the amount of fish you are allowed to keep per person per day.

Bail: the ring of metal positioned on a spinning reel. The bail is flipped open when you cast, then closed when you're fishing.

Bait: the food that you put on a hook to attract and ultimately catch a fish. These can be dead baits, like a chunk of fish or a raw mussel, or live baits such as smaller fish that attract larger predatory fish.

Barb: the bit that sticks out near the point of the hook. This helps secure the fish on the hook and stop the hook from coming out mid battle.

Barbless hook: a hook without a barb designed for catch and easy release.

Bird's nest: massive tangle in your fishing line. It's a nightmare and a high-anxiety moment.

Blind casting: trying to find where the fish are in unfamiliar water, often when fly fishing in deep pools or fast-moving water.

Blood and guts: fishing with bait as opposed to lures.

Boil-up: when bait fish school near the surface in the ocean, attracting all sorts of predatory fish and seabirds, including bombing gannets.

Brackish water: a mix of salt and fresh water, often formed where a river or creek flows into an estuary or directly into the sea.

Braid: a super-fine line that has little or no stretch. Designed for fishing in deeper water, braid is super sensitive so the angler can feel the lightest of bites.

Breaking strain: the point at which the line breaks when under pressure.

Burley: a type of bait to attract fish to a location. Usually made up of ground-up fish guts and the like, then frozen in blocks. When using frozen burley, place it in an onion sack or burley container so it drifts out into the current as it thaws — and make sure you attach a rope to pull it back in. This will attract the fish to the location of your baited hook offering.

Cast: the act of swinging a fishing rod, usually from behind your back and releasing the line at a certain point to propel the bait, lure and/or terminal tackle forward into the water.

Catch and release: the practice of catching a fish, handling it in the proper manner when removing the hook, then gently lowering it back into the water to swim away.

Change it up: if your set-up is not catching fish, try something else — perhaps a different lure or bait, or a lighter sinker . . .

Chum: another form of burley, where you chop up small pieces of fish or shellfish, then toss it into the current occasionally to attract the fish towards your baited hook.

Drag: a setting on the fishing reel that regulates the tension or force required for the fish to take line off the spool. The tighter the drag, the harder it is for the fish to run.

Drift fishing: when the boat you are fishing from is not under anchor. The current and the wind are pushing or pulling the boat along.

Drogue: a piece of canvas or similar, shaped like a cone, with a large opening at one end and a small opening at the other. Used to slow the boat or vessel down when drift fishing.

Drop-off: where the water goes from shallow to deep.

Eddy: a slow-moving piece of water next to faster-moving water, often creating a whirlpool.

Fish on: a popular saying when you have hooked and are playing a fish. For some reason, as soon as the words leave your mouth the fish often gets off.

Flasher rigs: rigs where the hooks have bright-coloured and sparkling materials attached to help entice the fish to bite.

Fluorocarbon: a type of fishing line that looks similar to nylon, but has better abrasion qualities, is invisible underwater (that's a good thing) and has less stretch. But you guessed it, it's more expensive too.

Foul: rocky terrain, usually underwater. Fish often hang around foul.

Foul-hooked: when you hook a fish anywhere in its body rather than in its mouth. It's sporting to release a foul-hooked fish.

Free spool: when you disengage the reel so there is no drag and the line can pull away with no tension. Also used for lowering terminal tackle to the bottom and for casting.

Gimbal belt: a padded belt that you put on, designed to transfer the weight and strain when fighting a large fish.

Harling: similar to trolling but done in lakes where a streamer fly is towed slowly just below the surface.

Hook: a bent piece of metal with a sharp end used to catch fish. (See page 54.)

Jig: a type of lure.

Leader: the frontmost section of the line that is connected to the mainline at one end and the hook or lure at the other end.

Leader knot: a knot that makes a strong connection between two lines.

Let it run: when you don't want to put too much pressure on the fish, often when you have a relatively light leader and you are worried that you will lose the fish as it will break your leader or pull the hook.

Lure: a small, artificial object used to attract fish, designed to mimic a smaller fish or insect, etc. (See page 56.)

Mainline: the main section of the fishing line that interacts with the rod and the reel.

Match the hatch: matching what the fish are eating with lures, flies or nymphs.

Monofilament: a type of fishing line often referred to as mono or nylon. It is made of a single fibre, and is probably the most common line used in recreational fishing.

Off the bricks: land-based fishing off the rocks.

Outrigger: poles on both sides of a boat that extend out at right angles, allowing you to fish lures at a range of distances from the vessel.

Oxbow: a crescent-shaped piece of water that appears in rivers.

Pillies: frozen pilchards.

Reel: a device used to store and wind fishing line by hand. There are all sorts of reels designed for specific rods and specific fishing styles. (See page 51.)

Retrieve: winding in the bait or lure towards you through the water.

Rig: your 'rig' is the combination of fishing tackle used to catch fish, such as the hooks, sinkers, lines, lures and swivels. (See page 65.)

Rod: a long, thin pole used to catch fish. There are lots of types of rod of different lengths and strengths, suited to different types of fishing. (See page 46.)

Rod action: the 'give' or bend in the rod (fast, medium, slow). Rods vary from stiff and heavy to ultra-light and bendy.

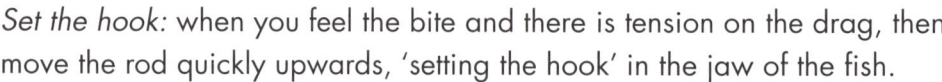

Set the hook: when you feel the bite and there is tension on the drag, then move the rod quickly upwards, 'setting the hook' in the jaw of the fish.

Sinker: a weight attached to a fishing line to sink the hook or lure and keep it in place. They also help to increase casting distance, and are usually made of lead. (See page 62.)

Skirt: rubber strands attached to various lures and hooks to make them more lifelike in the water.

Skunked: 'I got skunked' means you didn't land a fish.

Spooked: when a fish senses danger and darts off before you get a shot at it.

Spool: the part of the reel that holds the fishing line. It plays an important role in casting distance and smoothness.

Straylining: a method of fishing where your bait is presented as naturally as possible, using very little or no weight to let it drift through the water.

Strike: whipping the rod upwards to set the hook.

Swivel: a metal device that allows two different sections of line to rotate independently of each other, helping to prevent tangles.

Tackle: all your fishing gear, including rods, lines, hooks, lures, sinkers and so on. You can never have enough tackle!

Terminal tackle: refers to the set-ups or rigs, including hooks, sinkers, lures and so on at the business end of your line.

Tight lines!: good luck! Often said directly after you have said goodbye to another angler. It refers to staying connected to your terminal tackle, and keeping your line tight when you've hooked a fish.

Tippet: a thin line that attaches the leader to the fly. Only used in fly fishing.

Top water: fishing on top of the water (in both saltwater and freshwater fishing).

Trolling: towing lures or live bait fish slowly behind a moving boat.

Turn up your drag: when a fish is getting the better of you and is heading for some foul to try to break off. Turning up the drag makes it harder for the fish to run and take line.

Whopper stopper: a large heavy rod and reel set-up.

Wind knot: a knot that appears in your line, usually formed when casting, often when fly fishing in windy conditions. Re-tie as it greatly weakens the leader.

TIGHT LINES!

YOUR
LUCKY
FISHING
HAT

YOUR LUCKY FISHING HAT

Your fishing hat is nearly as important as any of the fishing gear you have in your tackle box. It pays to pick one that suits your personality and style and then stick with it. It's a well-known fact that the more you wear the same hat fishing, the more luck comes your way!

Over time, fishing hats get quite a distinctive odour (some may say 'stink') as layer upon layer of sweat builds up from those long hot days fishing under the 'big yellow'. The advantage of this is that no one in their right mind will ever try to steal yours.

Of course, it's not just your look that you have to think about. Choose a fishing hat that will protect you from the sun's harmful rays, with a decent brim to help cut the glare. Wearing a hat on your noggin when heading out fishing is not negotiable; it's as important as any other piece of kit or tackle. Here are a few options to try on for size.

TRUCKER CAP

More of a rural hard-core or truckie vibe, usually with a big logo like 'John Deere Tractors' splashed across the foam front panel. Mesh around the back will keep your nut cooler than a traditional baseball cap.

BASEBALL CAP

Very sports jock, with a small side of preppy. Baseball caps fade with time in the sun, and if you are constantly working the brim, you get a decent U-shape that looks pretty cool. The older they get, the better they wear. My choice.

BUCKET HAT

Bucket hats have a wild history — Gilligan (from *Gilligan's Island*, for any oldies out there) wore one constantly, as did Inspector Clouseau from *The Pink Panther*. The hip-hop community also embraced the bucket hat from around the 1980s as a symbol of urban culture. So, wearing a bucket hat basically covers gangster to goofball vibes and everything in between.

BEANIE

Everyone who fishes should take a beanie along; it's a necessary piece of kit that takes up little space and should be part of your gear list on any fishing trip. While the day may start out sunny and fine, nature has a habit of getting angry every so often and can turn cold, wet and windy extremely quickly. Keeping your dome warm in cold weather is essential.

FEDORA HAT

With their wide brim, indented crown and a pinched front, often made of felt, leather or straw, these timeless hats always seem a little upper-crust. They take a while to break in but when they do, a well-worn classic felt fedora certainly gives the wearer an air of self-confidence. Think Harrison Ford as Indiana Jones, Humphrey Bogart or even Al Capone.

NEWSBOY FLAT CAP

Popularised in the 1920s, these old-school woollen hats with a stiff peak visor at the front always shout 'sleeves rolled up' no-nonsense working class to me. The Shelby family from *Peaky Blinders* made them look pretty urban and super cool. A tweed version would be right at home if you're into fly fishing. Don't forget Brian Johnson, lead singer of AC/DC, was always rocking one (excuse the pun)!

FOREIGN LEGION CAP

While you will definitely look a bit 'boffin', the Foreign Legion get-up gives serious coverage for your neck. This is where the large section of material hanging out the back really comes into its own. Of course if you are sporting a decent mullet, you already have that covered. These hats are great to dip in water on a hot day, to cool your head, neck and back.

BRIXTON FIDDLER CAP

These hats can go one of two ways: you can end up looking like a slightly arrogant 747 pilot; or, if it's an old woollen version, you're going to look like 'Captain Sea Dog', as salty as they come.

FISHING KIT

YOUR FISHING KIT CAN BE AS SIMPLE OR AS COMPLEX AS YOU CHOOSE — THERE'S AN OPTION FOR EVERY FISHING SITUATION YOU CAN IMAGINE.

Here's the low-down on rods, reels, hooks, lures, sinkers and rigs — from just getting started right through to fishing level: extreme.

FISHING RODS

There is so much choice in fishing rods, with specialised fishing rods for different situations. It doesn't mean you have to have them all — start with one, and build up to a collection as you become more experienced. My recommendation is to 'buy once and buy right', by investing in a good-quality rod. If you look after your gear, it will look after you for decades. For that to happen, you need to give the rod a wash in soapy warm water after each fishing outing, then rinse with fresh water, especially if you have been fishing in salt water.

Many rods can be used for different styles of fishing. For instance, while you can purchase a specialised rod for targeting squid, you could also use a more general soft-bait rod set-up instead.

Fishers generally agree that there are seven styles of fishing rod. Most rods are made of three types of material: fibreglass, carbon or composite (a hybrid of fibreglass and carbon). If you are new to the sport, it pays to chat with people who know what they are talking about or with tackle shop staff. You will need to know what sort of fishing you are going to do and where you will be doing it.

Rods are also categorised by what sort of 'action' they deliver. This describes how much of the rod bends when you put pressure on the tip. A fast-action rod will bend only the top third, medium-action will bend the top half of the rod and slow-action will bend starting in the lower third of the rod.

'The fishing was good; it was the catching that was bad.'
— A. K. Best

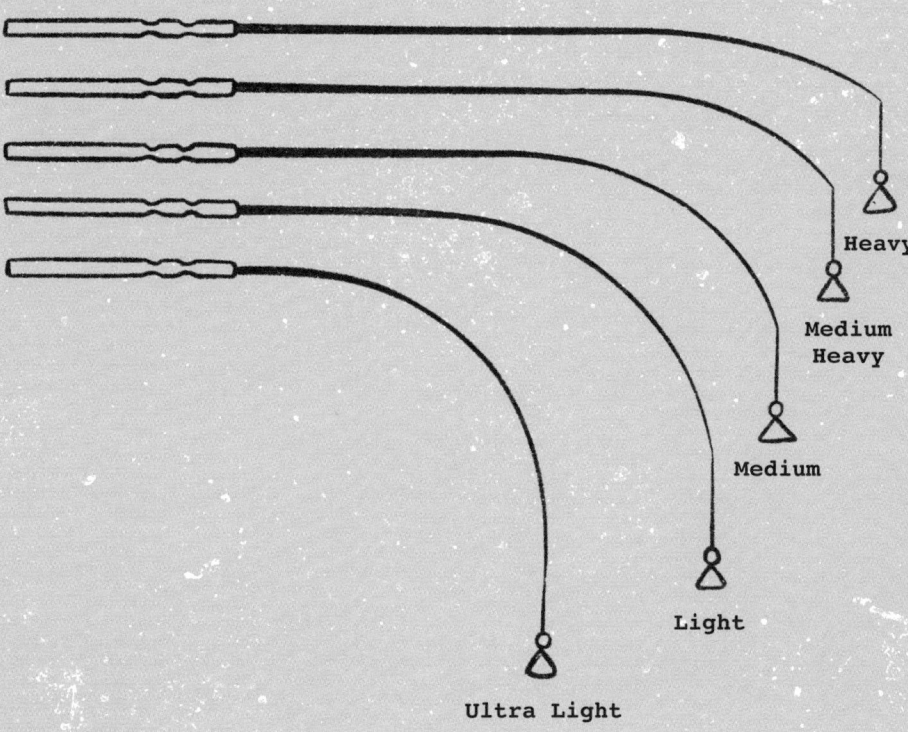

Power of the rod

1. Boat rods

A boat rod is probably the most common and versatile rod available, and is suited to people who love fishing ledger or flasher rigs, trolling and straylining. They range in weights: the really heavy boat rods are used for fishing big baits with large heavy sinkers targeting deep-water fish species like hāpuka, bass and bluenose. Boat rods are usually between 2 and 2.5 metres long. Although they are commonly fitted with a drum-style reel, you can set them up with spin and bait-runner reels too, so you can cast big baits like whole pillies and/or a kahawai head out the back of the boat when straylining for snapper.

2. Surfcasting rods

There's something about surfcasting that I have always loved. It's very popular in Aotearoa, especially with folks who don't have access to a boat. Surfcasting rods are large (anywhere from 3.6 metres to a massive 4.9 metres long) and relatively stiff, which gives you plenty of horsepower for a huge cast. These rods let you battle large snapper and kingfish and everything in between. It pays to also purchase a rod holder, which you can drive into the sand or wedge between some rocks, to save holding this big gear for hours.

3. Soft-bait rods

Soft-baiting is my favourite form of saltwater fishing. Soft-bait rods can be used in several situations: casting, trolling for trout and, at a pinch, fishing smallish jigs. They start at about 2 metres long, going up to around 2.6 metres, and most sit in the medium to fast action range. As they are a relatively light rod, fishing with them can be loads of fun, especially if you hook a decent-sized snapper or small(ish) kingi.

4. Top water rods

These heavy-duty rods are designed for casting as well as scrapping with large kingfish and the like, from the shore and the boat. When combined with a great-quality reel loaded with strong breaking strain braid, these rods will give you serious leverage when a big fish is taking charge. Top water fishing is becoming popular as you are constantly casting floating lures such as stick baits and poppers, then retrieving them along the surface. Seeing the fish chase your lure as you wind it in is serious heart-in-your-mouth stuff, when you see the chase then feel the weight come on. These rods are usually 2 to 2.6 metres long.

5. Ultra-light fishing rods

These ultra-light but super-strong fishing rods have really injected some serious fun into fishing. Growing up we had stiff boat rods, and while they did the job, there wasn't nearly as much excitement compared with fishing with light gear. Using an ultra-light rod, when paired with smallish overhead reels loaded with 4–10 kilogram braid, means you feel the softest of bites, and when you hook a fish the rod nearly bends in half, giving you some serious fun. These rods are great to fight tough customers like snapper, trevally and kahawai, and also trout. You can cast small lures with these rods too.

Many ultra-light rods break down into two pieces, so don't take up too much space if you are travelling. They range in length from around 1.5 to 1.8 metres. Of course, the longer the rod, the easier it is to cast long.

6. Telescopic or travelling rods

These lightweight rods are designed for travelling. The rods either break down to four or five pieces or are a retracting telescope style, making them compact, light and super portable for camping and tramping, strapped to your backpack. They range in size from around 1 to 3.5 metres long, with most fishers preferring something around the 2 to 3 metres mark.

7. Jig rods

Jig-style fishing is becoming very popular. There are a range of techniques; it pays to become good at one style to begin with and then purchase a rod and reel that suits that method. Jig rods are super light and strong for their length. Pay close attention to the manufacturer's instructions as to the maximum weight and drag the rod is designed for.

8. Fly-fishing rods

Fly fishing is one of my true loves. I've been freshwater fly fishing for trout for many years, and I've recently been introduced to the joys of fly fishing in salt water too. You can target nearly all the same fish species as with other rods; the difference is that you are presenting a fly, not bait or a lure.

While I have caught plenty of snapper, trevally and kahawai on a fly rod, I have yet to bag a legal-sized kingfish this way. However, I have seen my brother Jeremy lock horns and win against these hoodlums of the ocean using a fly. Extraordinary to witness!

Fly rods come in many weights, which generally indicate the size of fish you are targeting. If you're targeting a smaller fish, use a rod with a smaller weight, which allows better presentation when casting. Fly rods are pretty long, starting at around 2.7 metres and going up to about 4 metres. They generally break down to pieces, and are stored in well-protected rod tubes — these rods are relatively fragile, even when made of carbon fibre.

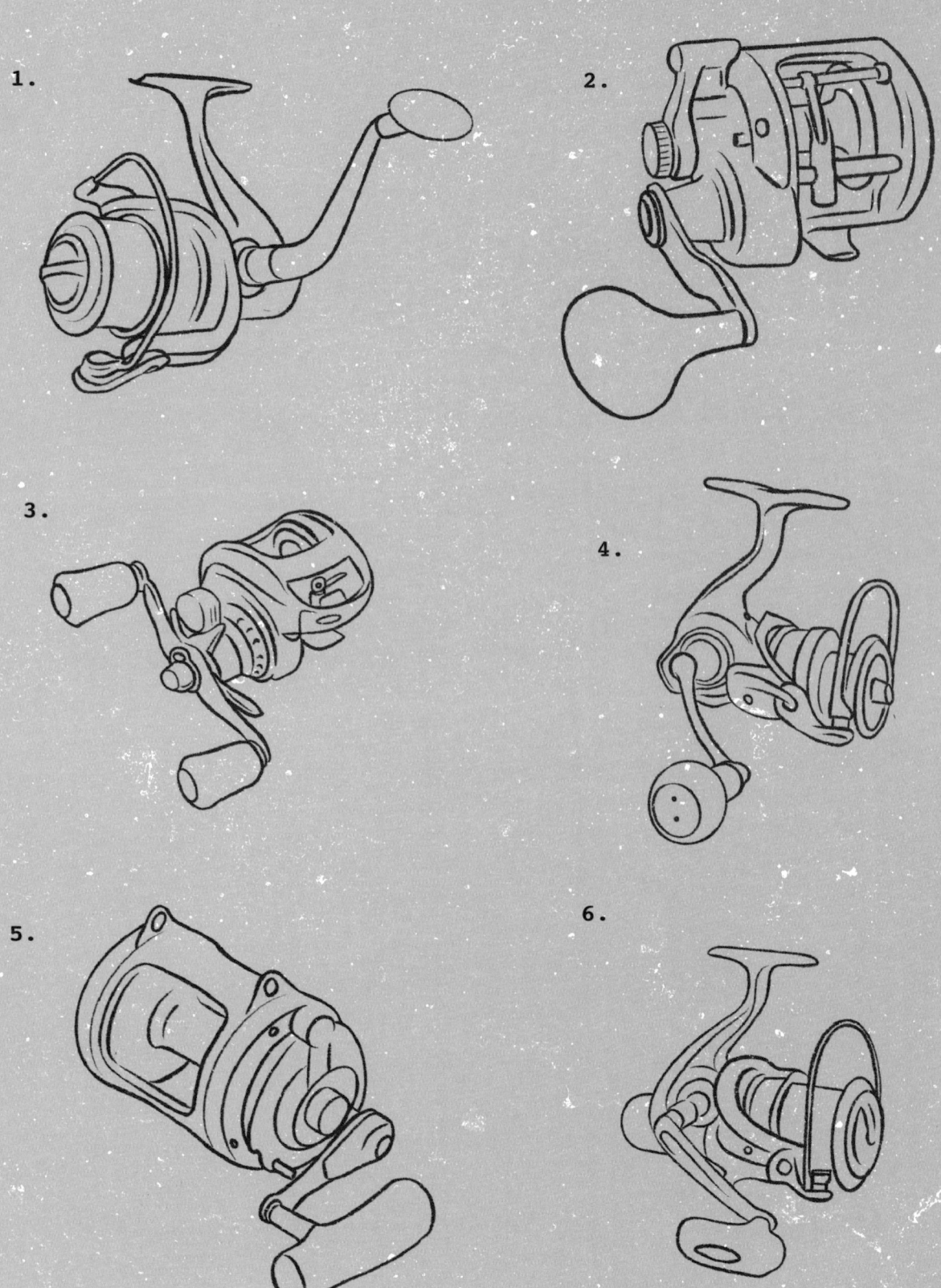

FISHING REELS

Fishing reels come in all shapes and sizes, each designed to suit a certain type of rod in different fishing environments. The biggest thing is to get the right combination of rod and reel. You'll need to consider the weight, drag and size of the reel; in general, the more you spend, the better the quality of the reel's inner components, which results in smoother drag systems when under serious load as you hook up a doozy.

It's important that you really look after your reels. If you thoroughly wash each reel (and rod) after every saltwater fishing mission and then spray them with a lubricant anti-rust liquid like CRC Tackleguard, your precious reels can last you a long time.

Here are the common types of reel you will encounter that will cover most fishing situations.

1. Spinning reels

These reels are super easy to use and you can use them in many different fishing situations. Spinning reels have a numbering system that starts at 500 and heads north past 20,000. The larger the number, the bigger the reel and the more line capacity. A reel in the range of 2500–6000 will suit most fishing situations, as it will have plenty of line for long casts and sturdy enough gears to fight a good-sized fish.

The gear ratios tell you how many full rotations the spool turns per rotation from the reel handle. So a 6:1 ratio means the spool of the reel will turn six times when the angler winds a full rotation of the handle. Flip the bail over to cast, and as soon as you start turning the reel handle the bail will automatically flip back.

2. Overhead reels

The overhead reel is a good old Kiwi favourite. These reels are designed for vertical fishing, which means you are dropping a line directly into the water below, perhaps from a boat or a wharf. Overhead reels are pretty versatile; they're perfect for baited ledger rigs, fishing with live bait or, if there is a bit of current, even straylining at a stretch. They're not really designed to be cast, but it's not impossible to put in an underhand cast out the back of the boat.

Overhead reels come in a range of sizes. They generally have room for a lot of line, which is useful for delivering heavily weighted terminal tackle in deepwater situations.

3. Baitcasting reels

I think baitcasting reels are really designed for more experienced anglers. They generally cast further and are more accurate for landing lures on the desired spot, but they take a bit of practice. Most of the newer models have an anti-reverse system built into the reel, but it can still be tricky to thumb the spool as line flows out when casting.

I have struggled to get on top of this sort of reel at times, and have too often ended up with a bird's nest of tangled line. Having said that, lots of anglers find these reels fantastic for slow and regular jigs.

4. Soft-bait reels

Soft-bait reels are very similar to the look and feel of a spinning reel. However, they generally have a bigger spool, allowing for a longer cast, and retrieval of the line is quicker with each rotation of the reel handle. With constant casting, soft-bait reels get a real workout each time you head out on a mission. My advice is to purchase the best you can afford and remember to wash it down with hot soapy water after each use, then spray it with CRC Tackleguard solution each time.

'Nothing makes a fish bigger than almost being caught.'
— Anonymous

5. Game-fishing reels

This is 'big dog' gear for catching ocean-going gamefish. Regular gear will not cut it in this arena. Whichever reel you choose needs to be a perfect match for a heavy-duty rod. The reels are large and heavy when fully spooled up with 24 kilogram monofilament — a large marlin's first run may be 300 or 400 metres long. Your reel also needs plenty of grunt to lever up and lift a large fish that has gone deep on you.

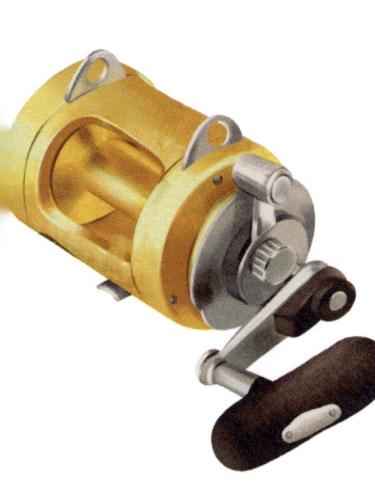

These reels are expensive as they have seriously smooth and efficient drag systems. The lever drag systems allow for very precise drag adjustments. This is no environment for compromise: the quality of tackle is the difference between catching or losing the fish of a lifetime. That's all I have to say on the matter.

6. Surfcasting reels

These large spinning reels are designed to cast long-distance. Once again it's a 'you get what you pay for' situation. Surfcasting often takes place in harsh environments, like windswept beaches or off rugged rocky outcrops along the coast.

HOOKS

While fish can be captured in a bunch of ways, like in different types of nets, various traps and pots and so on, I would guess that most fish landed recreationally are caught on a hook of some sort. In the last couple of decades or so, there have been vast improvements on the basic hooks we used to fish with in the past. These days, chemically sharpened hooks that you would describe as 'needle sharp' have improved hook-up and catch rates dramatically.

The variety of hooks that are on the market is mind-boggling. Smaller, finer, super-tough hooks are also becoming popular when combined with relatively heavy lures designed to catch large fish. With such an array of choice these days, it pays to ask the tackle shop assistants for their advice around which hooks would be ideal for the fish you are targeting and with the fishing gear you have at your disposal.

Following are the common styles of hooks that will cover most New Zealand fishing situations. They all come in multiple sizes and of course different price points. My advice is to purchase the best you can afford — often it makes all the difference!

1. Circle hooks

The circle hook, as the name suggests, is in the shape of three-quarters of a circle with the sharp pointed barb nearly pointing back at the shank of the hook. Circle hooks have become very popular as the hook inevitably ends up in the side of the fish's mouth, which significantly cuts down on fish mortality by eliminating the risk of them being hooked in the gut.

Circle hooks are easy to dislodge, which means you can limit the time and stress placed on a landed fish that you are planning to release. When fishing with circle hooks, be aware that when you feel the bite, it's best to simply begin winding the reel, as opposed to striking (jerking the rod) in the traditional way, as that sometimes pulls the baited hook clear out of the fish's mouth.

2. Barbless hooks

Barbless hooks are also popular, especially with the 'catch and release' crowd. It's all about looking after a landed fish quickly and with as little stress for the fish as possible before releasing it back into the water. While a barb helps secure and land a hooked fish, a fisher worth their salt will land just as many fish with a barbless hook through skill and knowledge they've obtained by battling with a hooked fish. If you keep constant pressure and contact on the line, it's virtually impossible to lose the fish.

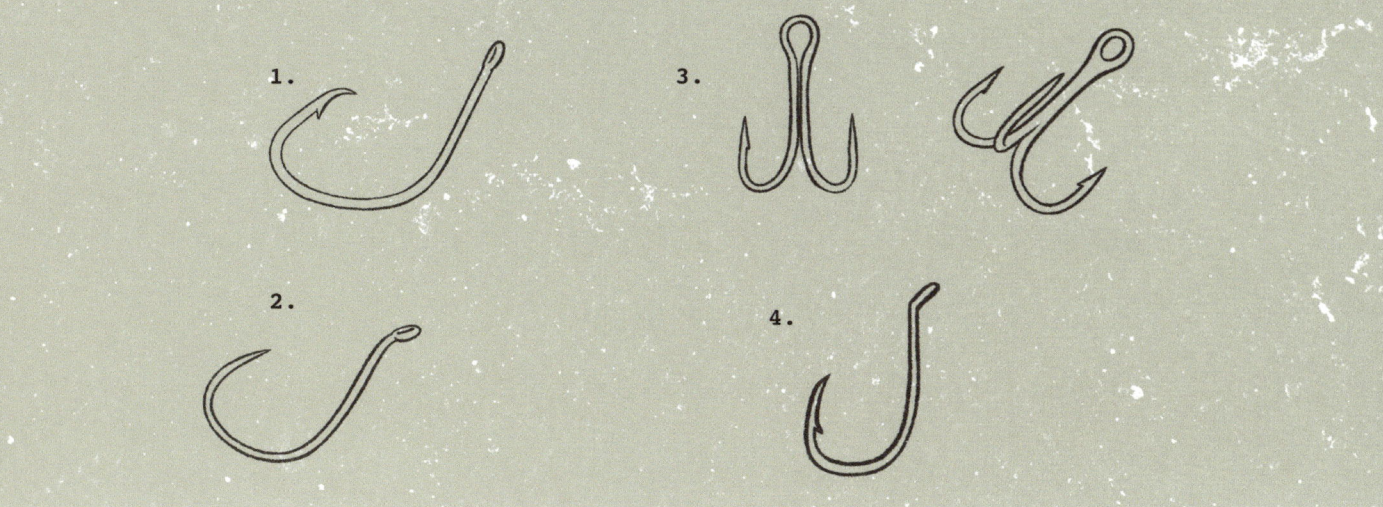

You can buy barbless hooks, or you can just crimp the barbs on regular hooks flat with a pair of pliers. Another reason to use a barbless hook is if you accidentally hook yourself, it comes out easily. A hook with a barb . . . not so much.

3. Double and treble hooks

A double hook has two points, and, you guessed it, a treble hook has three. These hooks are mostly used as terminal tackle attached to hard-body lures, such as top water stick baits and trolling lures. Be very careful when handling them if there are two sets on one lure, especially if you are handling a hooked and landed fish that is thrashing about. A treble hook attached to some part of your body is not fun at all. You can also purchase barbless double and treble hooks.

4. 'J' hooks

As the name suggests, J hooks are made in the shape of the letter J. There are a few variations, such as the 'offset' J hook, where the tip or pointy end of the hook doesn't line up with the straight shank of the hook. These hooks are designed to better secure the bait, and in theory, they are more likely to hook the fish. The downside is that an offset hook is also more likely to gut-hook the fish, which increases the mortality of smaller fish and fish you had intended to release.

The 'beak' hook is another type of J hook. Also known as octopus beak hooks or suicide hooks, beak hooks are a very popular choice with New Zealanders as they work well on many of our common species such as snapper, gurnard and blue cod. The gape of the hook (the distance between the point and the shank) is wider in relation to the length of the hook than other hooks. The beak hook also has an extra-long point. These hooks are great for strip baits and whole or half pilchards.

LURES

A lure is a small, artificial object with protruding hooks that is tied onto the leader. It mimics smaller fish or bait fish. There are literally thousands of fishing lures to choose from, for all types of fishing. Fishing with lures, especially in salt water, continues to become more and more popular. There are a few reasons for this:

- Apart from trolling lures, most lure fishing is active fishing with different techniques around casting and retrieving. It pays to learn a few techniques, as often one works better than another on certain days. If the fishing is slow, always change it up.
- With fly fishing, I think it feels more skilful and satisfying to fool, hook and land a fish with an imitation of a smaller fish or insect.
- Lastly, the other massive bonus to lure fishing is you are not dealing with a 'stinky bait' situation.

1. Gamefish lures

There is no 'sure bet' when it comes to gamefish lures — what worked well yesterday or last year could be a dud tomorrow. Gamefish lures come in many sizes, colours, weights and shapes. Some have different heads, and longer and shorter skirts. If you are going to get into game fishing, my advice is to just start purchasing the odd lure here and there to build up a collection over the years.

All lures swim a little differently, depending on their makeup, where they are positioned in the wake of the boat, the speed the vessel is travelling and so on. Gamefish lures range from cheap to expensive, but I don't think the more expensive ones give you a better chance of hooking up. I've heard of someone towing a jandal with a hook attached and catching a marlin on it!

2. Soft baits

I simply love soft-baiting and I fish this way nearly 80 percent of the time, mainly from my kayak in shallow water targeting hopefully enormous snapper. While basic versions date back to the 1950s, the soft baits that were developed in the 1990s, with their very fishy action, was when soft-baiting really took off.

Like all lures, soft baits come in a range of sizes, colours and shapes. You purchase the soft baits separately to weighted jig head hooks, which lets you mix and match the lure and the hook. The general rule is that the deeper the water you are fishing in, the heavier the weighted jig head.

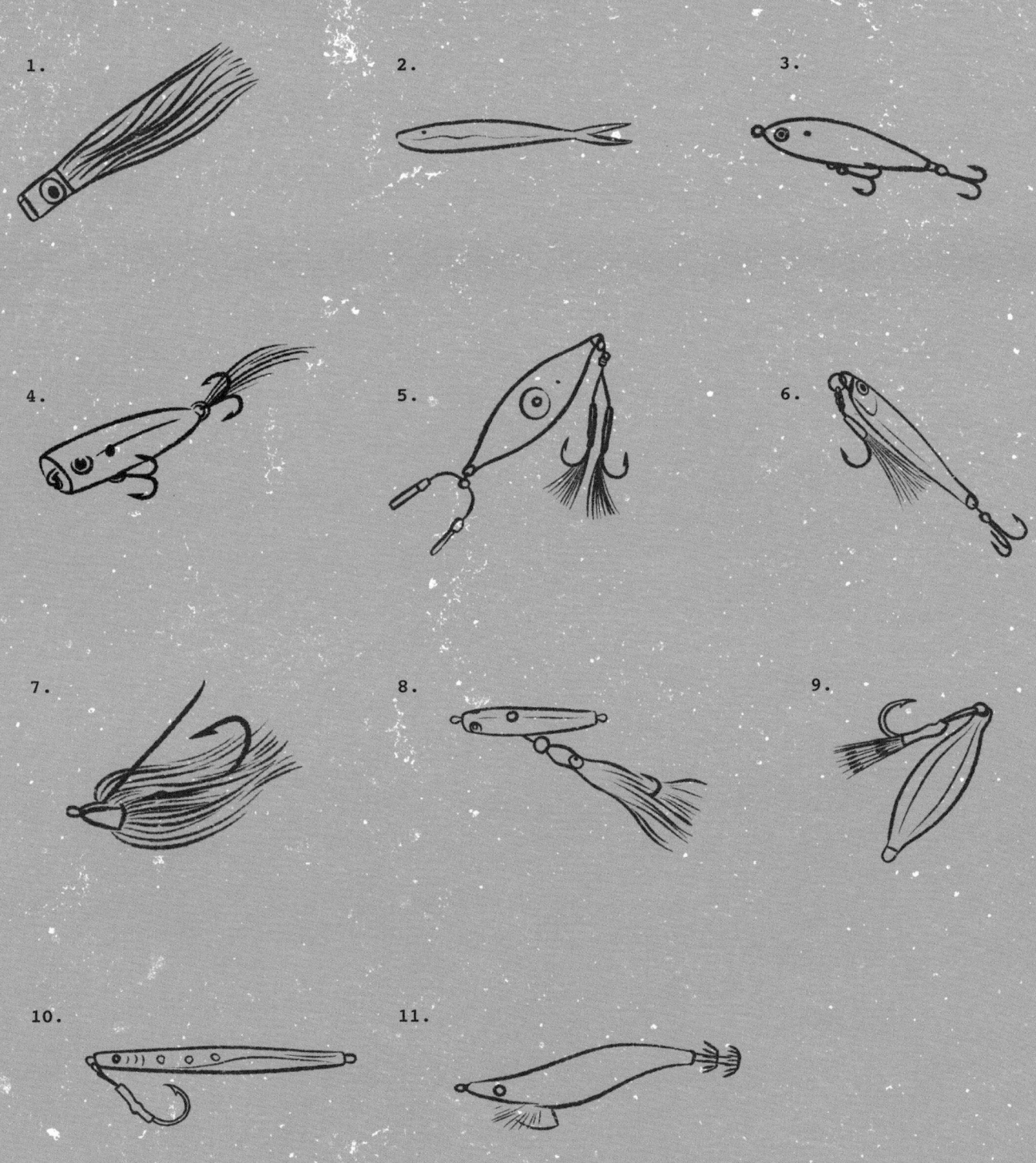

To fish soft baits, cast away from yourself, generally up-current so when it lands, the soft bait comes back towards you in the current. Fish will take the soft bait when it hits the water, when it is working its way down through the water column, and often when it swings back and is directly under you. Your fishing line should be braid with a leader of around 1.5 metres. This is a fun way to fish as you are working the lures constantly, prospecting different water as you go. Fish with a light purpose-made soft-bait casting rod and the correct matching reel, and stand back and enjoy some serious rod-bending adrenalin-filled action.

Remember, it is important to stay connected to your soft bait, as the fish can strike from the moment the soft bait lands in the water.

3. Stick baits

Stick baits are hard-bodied baits that are designed to imitate a wounded fish. Traditionally made from hand-carved wood and often referred to as 'kingfish candy', they are used in top-water lure fishing. This is incredibly exciting fishing as it is breathtakingly visual; you see the fish chase the lure, which sure gets your heart pumping.

Stick baits are designed to be cast from relatively stiff rods with high-quality reels. An expert caster will be able to cast the stick bait up to 80 metres before beginning the retrieve. The fisher will use a sweeping style of motion when retrieving the lure, so the stick bait moves through the water then appears to hesitate, then moves again.

Stick baits are often set up with two treble hooks attached, one in the tail and one attached to the belly of the lure. Often when retrieving the stick bait you can have a number of fish chasing the lure as it works its way back to you — and when you hook up, get ready, as you'll have a serious battle on your hands.

4. Poppers

Very similar to a stick bait, a popper has a cupped or moulded front to imitate the movement of fish on the top of water.

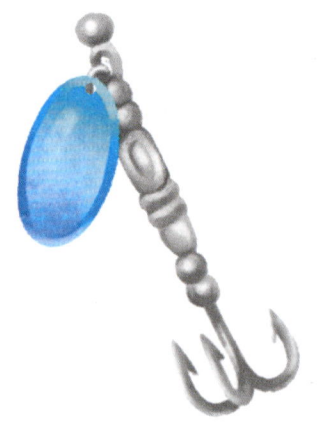

Used in a similar way to a stick bait, the popper will give you the same thrill from actually seeing the fish chase then hopefully grab the lure as you work the lure on the retrieve after the cast.

5. Slow-pitch jigs

Slow-pitch jigs are relatively new on the scene, developed by crazy-good anglers from Japan. Fishing with these jigs is definitely a bit more difficult to master, but after some practice you're going to love this slow form of jigging and catch many fish this way. 'Pitch' means one full wind of the reel. The action comes more from the lift and drop of the rod, which causes the lure to flutter down, making it look too enticing even for a lazy fish to ignore. You'll need a rod and reel also suited to slow-pitch jig to fish these lures effectively.

6. Spinners

Spinners are metal lures that come in all sorts of shapes, sizers and colours, and are designed to imitate bait fish. Used mainly in salt water, they also work well in rivers and lakes when targeting trout or salmon. A spinner lure is either cast and retrieved, or trolled. The spinner lure is often rigged with a single hook or very thin sharp treble hooks. To fish spinners, you need a light casting rod and reel set-up that will give you a heap of fun when you are hooked up, especially when targeting feisty kahawai.

7. Sliding-head lures

Called sliding or kabura lures, these lures arrived on the scene only a few years ago. They have a heavy head that often looks like a big eye, and are designed to imitate a small fish or octopus moving just above the ocean floor.

The leader runs through the centre of this heavy weight and there are two deadly sharp hooks hidden in the rubber skirt that trails behind. These lures can be used in all sorts of depths: the deeper the fish, the heavier the head. Sometimes you'll catch fish when it's heading down, as the rubber skirt which flutters down behind the weight is very enticing to fish.

Once it catches up to the weighted head on the bottom, the angler deliberately and relatively slowly winds the lure up then drops it back to the sea floor. The fish will hook themselves by attacking the lure. These are a great learner lure for people who don't fish a lot, as they are easy to use and can be very deadly when the bite is on.

8. Inchiku jigs

A jig is a weighted fishing lure. Like sliding head lures, inchiku jigs can be effective especially when being worked under birds and around boil-ups. You can fish these in varying depths of water, using lighter jigs in shallow, heavier in deep.

Attach your leader to the jig with the hooks hanging below, hidden in the rubber tassels. Drop the inchiku lure to the bottom, then slowly start winding it up until you get a bite in the zone where the fish are holding, which is usually within the first 20 metres from the sea bottom. Repeat the process by releasing into free-spool to drop the inchiku jig back to the bottom until you hook up.

It pays to keep a slow, steady wind when you feel the bite, as opposed to a sharp, fast strike. I have had a lot of fun and success fishing these types of lures; keep a few different weights and colours in your tackle kit.

9. Micro jigs

Micro jigs are small jigs with single hooks that are super fun to fish with. They range in weight from about 5 to 40 grams, but the 20-gram mark would be the most popular. They are fished like a soft bait, where you cast forward of your position, fishing the lure down through the water column then intermittently winding the lure back towards you. Wind up, then cast again. They cast like a bullet, especially those constructed of super-heavy tungsten. Fished from light but strong rods, they often catch a huge variety of fish. Even though they are micro, you can still catch some 'stonkers' — big fish seem to love these micro jig lures.

'It doesn't matter if the rod is or isn't bent. Time spent fishing is time well spent.'
— Justin Morgan

10. Speed jigs

Speed jigs are seriously heavy-duty terminal tackle. They are designed for deeper water fishing. While a slow jig action flutters down to represent a wounded fish, the speed jig is retrieved through the water column at high speed, imitating a fleeing fish. This is another challenging type of fishing to learn, but when you master the action required to tempt the bite, you are in for a lot of fun. It is a combination of winding and working the rod at the same time. My suggestion is to master the art of speed jigging with someone who is good at the technique, before forking out the dollars for the correct rod and reel set-up for this style of jigging. A gimbal belt nearby will also be an asset, as hooking a super-large kingi or a big bass will just about pull your arms out of your shoulder sockets.

11. Squid jigs

Fresh squid is probably my favourite seafood to eat, which is a big call but I stand by it. I like to target a species called broad squid, which are an absolute delicacy. Winter is the season they move inshore to spawn, and while some say squid fishing is best at night, my most productive sessions have been in the middle of the day.

Squid jigs come in all weights, sizes and colours, and it pays to have a bunch, as what worked well yesterday won't necessarily catch today. The way you fish the jigs is called egging. Cast the jig as far as possible, letting it drift slowly down through the water column, and when you think it is near the sea bottom, jerk the rod rapidly three or four times, winding a bit as you go, then let it drift down again. Repeat until the jig is back at your feet. It takes a bit of practice to master this.

Squid don't fight in the same way as a fish; it is more of a heavy tug. There are no barbs on a squid jig, so you must keep the pressure on the whole time. It pays to have a net, as many get away when you're retrieving them out of the water. Be warned: they also often squirt jet-black ink a couple of times, either in the water or, unfortunately, out of the water, on you and everything else lying about.

SINKERS

A sinker does just what you would expect: it takes your terminal tackle down to the ocean floor. Selection of a suitable sinker is often an afterthought, but it pays to consider whether you have the right sinker for the type of fishing you're doing. Usually the best results are achieved when your sinker is just heavy enough to get the bait or the lure in the desired spot to catch fish. The right style of sinker along with the right amount of weight can be the difference between a slow day and an absolute ripper.

Tips for selecting a sinker

- Choose the correct type of sinker for the style of fishing you are carrying out.
- The water's depth and strength of current determines what weight of sinker to use.
- A sinker with the right weight will position your bait as naturally as possible in the strike zone.
- Less is usually more. If the sinker is too heavy, the fish is more likely to feel the weight and spit the bait out.
- Be prepared to change the weight of the sinker when conditions change, such as the current beginning to run faster. Don't set and forget.

1. Fixed or stationary sinkers

This type of sinker is used a lot in deeper water, where it will anchor itself in a chosen spot. Ideal for a ledger rig or flasher rig.

2. Ball or egg sinkers

These sinkers have a hole through their middle. They are designed so the line runs though the weight without the fish feeling any resistance. They are ideal for straylining rigs.

3. Clip-on sinkers

These sinkers have a metal loop and are designed to be changed out quickly and efficiently. They are ideal for ledger rigs and dropper rigs.

4. Split-shot sinkers

These are very small weights that you can crimp on to a line to add small amounts of weight. They are ideal for fly fishing and for adding minimal weight to any rig.

5. Breakaway sinkers

These sinkers are made especially for surfcasting over sand. They are ideal for ledger rigs.

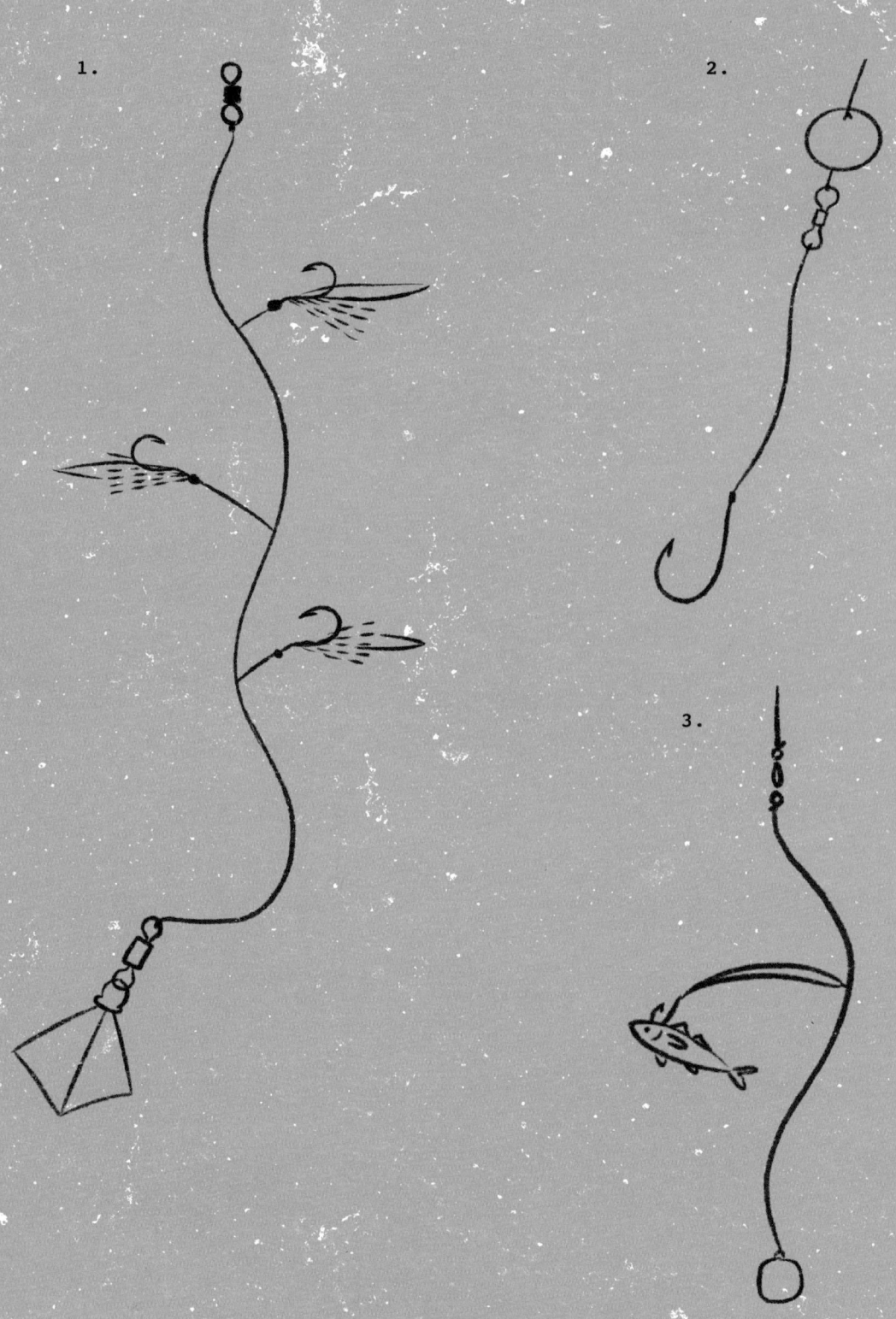

SALTWATER FISHING RIGS

A fishing rig is a combination of fishing tackle items — the equipment at the end of your fishing line. The following rigs will cover most fishing situations in New Zealand.

1. Ledger or dropper rigs

This rig is probably the most common saltwater fishing rig in New Zealand. It's mainly used for fishing off the bottom, and it consists of a mainline with a couple of droppers attached (around 25 centimetres apart), then a weighted sinker at the bottom. The droppers have a hook attached to each one, which means you're essentially fishing at slightly different depths. It's a highly effective rig that covers most bottom-dwelling varieties of fish.

2. Running rigs

This popular rig is often used when there is quite a bit of current running. It has a relatively heavy ball sinker on the mainline side of the swivel, then the leader and one or two hooks on the end. The ball sinker sits on the ocean floor, and the bait floats naturally behind.

3. Deepwater live bait rigs

This rig is similar to a dropper or ledger rig, where the sinker is on the bottom of a relatively heavy leader. The deepwater live bait rig has one dropper with a circle hook for the live bait to be hooked onto. The leader then goes up to a swivel that is attached to the mainline. This is a pretty deadly set-up to catch any bottom-dwelling predatory fish.

'The charm of fishing is that it is the pursuit of what is elusive but attainable, a perpetual series of occasions for hope.'
— John Buchan

4. Top water live bait with balloon

This rig has a balloon instead of a sinker. A single circle hook is tied to the bottom of a heavy leader that leads up to a swivel which the mainline is attached to. The balloon is tied to the top half of the swivel. This rig keeps the live bait fish just under the surface of the water, waiting for an unsuspecting hungry kingfish to turn up.

5. Sabiki rigs

Sabiki rigs have about six tiny hooks connected to about a 50 centimetre leader, and generally come made up from the manufacturer. They are used vertically for small bait fish, like slimy and jack mackerel, piper, sprat and herring. It can be quite a faff to fish with six small hooks flying around, so I tend to cut them in half and fish just three hooks, which reduces the risk of tangles and annoying little hooks sticking into you.

These rigs are an important piece of kit for any fisho who is into live-bait fishing. Sabiki rigs make it relatively easy to catch lots of bait fish quickly and efficiently, filling your live bait tank so you can head out to target the larger species. They are great rigs for fishing off a wharf, too. A tiny piece of bait such as squid will increase the effectiveness of fishing with a sabiki rig.

I think we often overlook how delicious these small fish are — they're good for more than just bait. I love eating herring, piper and mackerel.

'If people concentrated on the really important things in life, there'd be a shortage of fishing poles.'
— Doug Larson

KNOTS
AND
NOTS

KNOTS AND NOTS

When it comes to fishing, it's hard to think of many things more important than being able to properly tie a bunch of knots. I've heard it said that the two keys to consistent fishing success are sharp hooks and a strong, well-tied knot. While there are numerous knots out there, you probably only need to learn about half a dozen max.

Knots only fail for two reasons: either they slip when under pressure from the weight or pulling power of the fish, or the knot was roughly constructed in the first place, which can result in one part of the line cutting through another part.

Start by learning a couple of knots that are relevant to the fishing method you enjoy the most. It's better to know a few knots that you can rely on to cover most situations than trying to learn too many at the same time. Knowing 'sort of how' to tie a particular knot won't cut it when you're under pressure.

Most anglers have experienced losing a fish (often a large one) when they discover a curly pig's tail at the end of their line. The sad truth is the knot wasn't good enough. It is a truly gut-wrenching moment that I have unfortunately experienced a number of times. While thankfully it happens to me a little less often these days, it usually occurs when I'm in a hurry or over-excited. Maybe I've just spotted a trout slurping insects off the surface of the river, or there is a boil-up with gannets diving in the ocean, or I'm experiencing a red-hot bite time.

Check your knots and leader regularly for any signs of nicks, abrasions or wind knots. Always re-tie your knots if there is any sign of wear and tear or wind knots; if you don't, your next cast and hook-up is highly likely to end in tears.

'Fishing is a discipline in patience. It's about the journey, not just the destination.'
— Chris Campanioni

It really pays to keep calm and not rush when you're tying your knots. Slow down, be deliberate and focus on tying the right knot correctly. If, for instance, the knot requires five loops, that's for a reason and just making three or four is not good enough.

Once you have pulled your knot up tight, always check that it holds by testing it with some strain on it.

The good thing is that learning to tie knots is so satisfying. It's something you can practise just about anywhere, and knowing a few knots will serve you well for the rest of your life. Keep some twine or fishing line handy, and try to get into the habit of practising when you are relaxing, like in front of the telly.

It's a good idea to start with relatively thick cord so it's easier to tie and undo. This way, you can see how the knot works and pulls up tight. Different-coloured cords are also useful to see what's going on when you're tying two separate lines together.

Once you're feeling more confident about your knot-tying skills, start practising with thinner lines, and then try the knots with the fishing tackle you'll use to fish with.

The materials for knot-tying are usually monofilament nylon, fluorocarbon or braid. Monofilament is a good choice for beginners, as it's a bit cheaper and easier to handle.

Here's an important tip — always remember to spit a little saliva on your knot before you pull it tight. This helps to eliminate the heat from the friction of pulling the knot tight. It makes your knots stronger (apparently by 12 percent!), which could be the difference between catching the fish of a lifetime or a nightmare story of 'the one that got away'.

TYPES OF KNOT

Here are six knots that will serve you well in most situations. You'll find lots of videos on YouTube that will walk you through each knot step by step. Just keep practising your knots until they become second nature and you can just about tie them in your sleep. Tight lines!

1. Blood knot

Often used when fly fishing, the blood knot is ideal for tying two lines of similar size together, such as two pieces of monofilament. This knot is a favourite because it keeps most of the line's original strength.

1.

5x

5x

Hold here

2.

3.

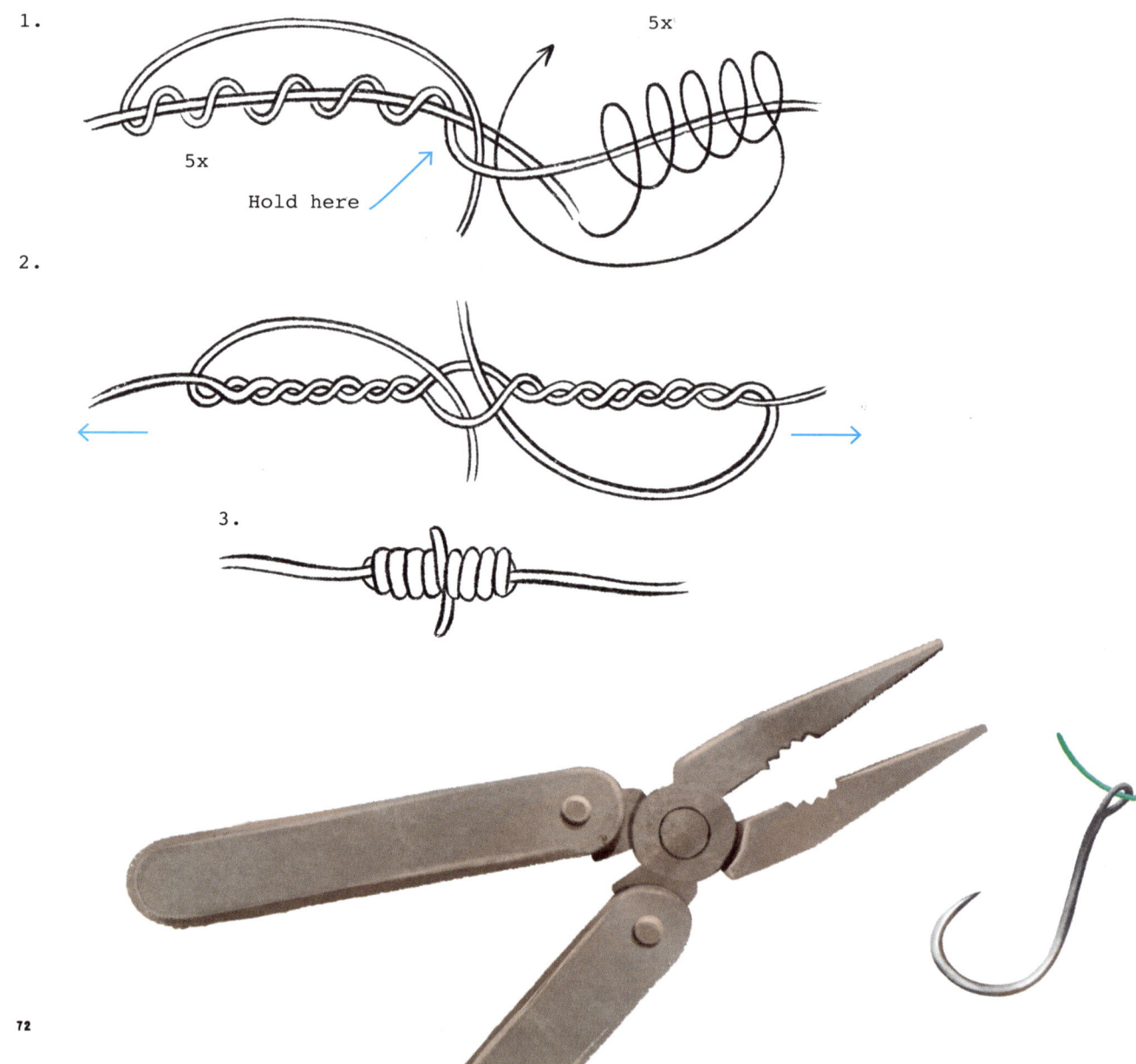

2. Half blood knot

The half blood knot is a relatively easy one to learn. It's very reliable, and is mainly used for attaching hooks, clips, swivels and the like to the line. The tag or working end is the end of the line you're winding around, threading through and so on while you keep the other end steady.

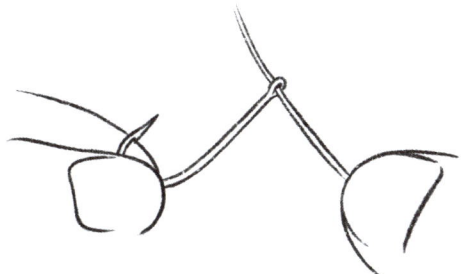

1. Thread the line through the eye

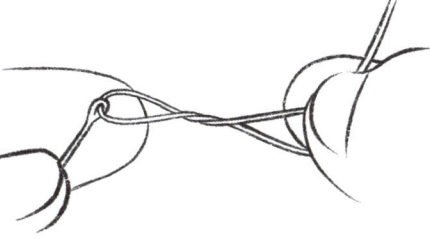

2. Make five turns of the tag around line

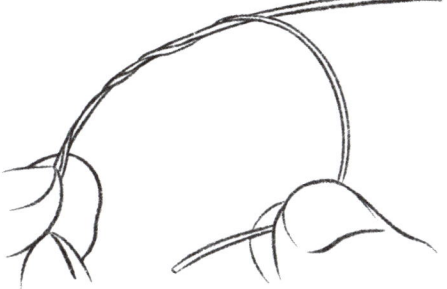

3. Take tag back to turn nearest eye

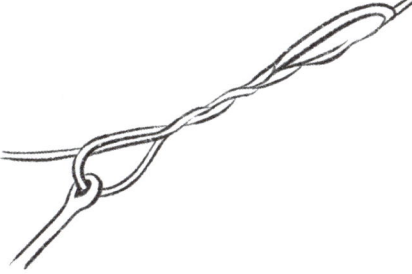

4. Pass tag through loop and lubricate

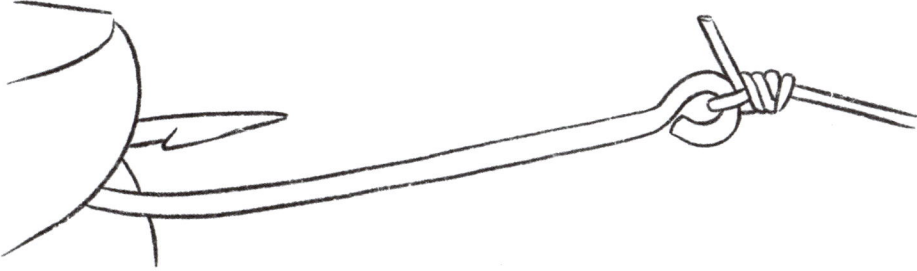

5. Pull the knot tight and trim off tag end close to the knot

3. Surgeon's loop knot

The surgeon's loop knot is a good one to use when you want to attach a lure or fly to the end of a line. It helps to make the lure or fly float in a way that seems natural to the fish. It's a strong knot, and it's pretty easy to tie too.

1.
2.
3.

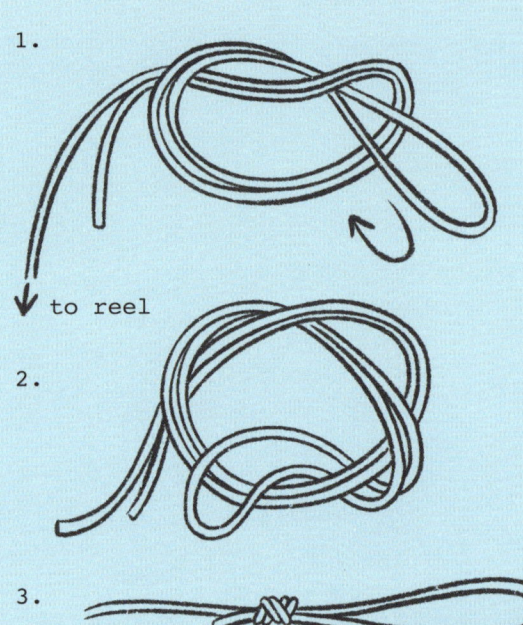

to reel

4. Improved clinch knot

The improved clinch knot is used mainly to secure hooks, swivels and lures to a line. It's popular because it's easy to tie.

1.

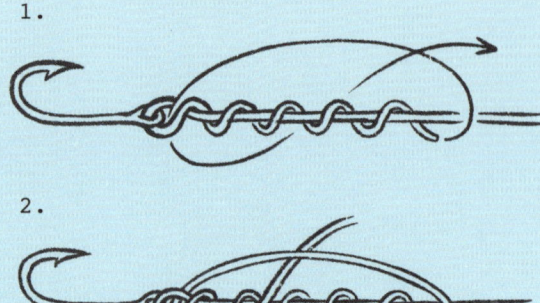

2.

5 – 6 wraps

3.

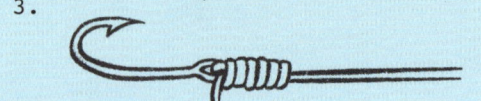

5. Double uni knot

The double uni knot is useful for tying two different types of line together, such as tying monofilament to braid.

1.

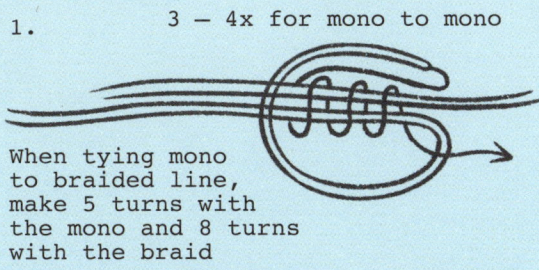

3 – 4x for mono to mono

When tying mono to braided line, make 5 turns with the mono and 8 turns with the braid

2.

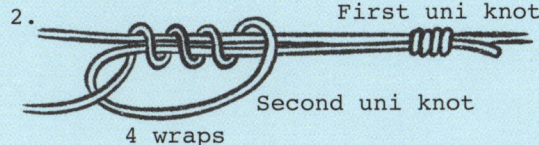

First uni knot
Second uni knot
4 wraps

3.

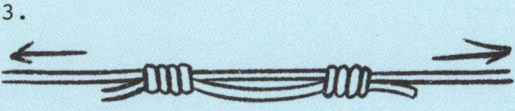

4.

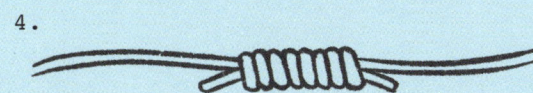

6. Lefty's loop knot

For folks like me that love to soft-bait, this is our 'go to' knot when tying a jig head to the leader. Like the surgeon's loop knot, it helps present the soft bait to the fish as naturally as possible.

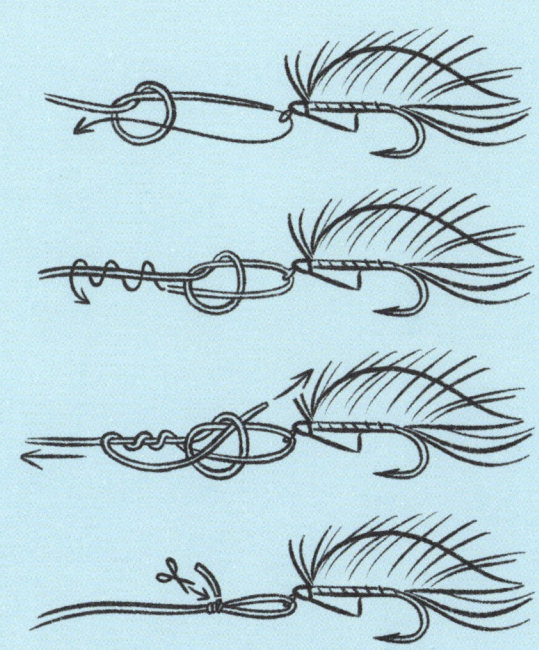

SAFETY IS NO ACCIDENT

When we're excited about going fishing, we're full of anticipation and our minds are focused on a fun day ahead. But keeping safe while you're fishing is always your top priority — it doesn't matter how many fish you catch if you don't come home safely at the end of the day.

Before you get anywhere near the water, make sure you read through this list. If there's something you and the adult helping you don't understand, find someone who can explain it to you — your local fishing club or fishing supplies shop might be a good place to start.

I reckon it's worth copying out this checklist — you can stick it on the wall by the door or even get it laminated and make it part of your fishing kit. You can also add other safety reminders that are specific to your fishing equipment and environment.

BEFORE YOU GO

Always check the latest weather forecast. If the weather is looking iffy, think about putting your fishing trip off for another day.

Tell someone where you are intending to fish and what time you plan to be home.

Check your equipment. Make sure your boat, kayak, outboard motors, etc are properly maintained and serviced, and that your lifejackets are in good condition.

Always check the tides

Talk to your adult fishing buddy about joining the Coastguard — there are all sorts of benefits from being a member and they save lives too! If you're out on the water, always log a trip report using the Coastguard app.

Do you have enough fuel for your trip? A back-up tank?

If you're going to be fishing in the dark, inspect your fishing spot in the daytime and identify likely hazards.

Communications

Take two forms of communication with you.

Pack a phone with decent battery life and keep it in a waterproof container.

Even better, pack an EPIRB (Emergency Position-Indicating Radio Beacon). I reckon they are worth every penny — $500 to save a life seems a good deal to me. You can also hire EPIRBs from outdoor-equipment shops.

A marine VHF radio is highly recommended for emergency communications out on the water. Use 'Channel 16' for emergencies.

What to pack
- Plenty of protection from the sun and the wind, including waterproof sunscreen (minimum SPF 30), sunglasses and a brimmed hat.
- Extra warm clothes, including a beanie, a jumper and a waterproof jacket. The weather can change rapidly and you need to make sure you don't get cold or wet.
- First-aid kit, including insect repellent.
- Flares.
- Water to drink and snacks to eat. You'll need them to stay hydrated and keep your energy up.

WHEN YOU'RE FISHING

If you're on a boat, make sure everyone has a lifejacket and is wearing it.

Your footwear must be suitable for the environment you are intending to fish from. Are you fishing from a boat, a rock ledge, a wharf . . . ?

Keep your fingers clear of the mouth of any fish. You'd be surprised how strong their bite can be.

Keep hooks and lures stored safely away in a tackle box.

When fishing from the shore and there is a swell running, never turn your back on the sea.

Always respect the captain or skipper's call.

Staying safe is your number-one job when you're fishing — remember, the fish will still be there tomorrow!

FISHING

FROM A

WHARF

FISHING FROM A WHARF

There's no doubt fishing is one of the most popular pastimes in our terrific little country. With such a massive coastline and so many places where you can 'wet a line', New Zealand is a great place to learn how to fish.

You can bet that with every salty adventure with a hook involved, you will learn something new, adding more knowledge to your fishing kete. And the very best place to start your fishing odyssey is at your local wharf.

While the gear may be smaller in size, many fishing situations in the future will most likely involve a rod, a line, hooks, swivels, sinkers and bait. Generally all these components just get a bit bigger as you start to target larger fish.

The first good thing about fishing from a wharf is that it is a great stable environment to fish from. It is also often a very social spot, where you can observe and interact with other anglers, young and old.

My suggestion is to ask someone with fishing experience to join you on your first couple of missions off the wharf. Most fishers love any sort of fishing and get a big buzz from sharing their knowledge and teaching you some good fishing habits to take on board.

You will learn so much even on your first outing, and these lessons will serve you well on all your fishing experiences well into the future. You will learn how to tie your first knot, how to bait a hook, how a fishing reel works, how to cast and how to release a fish — or, if you are keeping them to eat or for bait, how to end a fish's life in a quick and humane way. Also, very importantly, you will learn how to look after your catch.

There may also be things you have not thought about. What is the forecast? What time is low tide? Which footwear is good to wear when fishing from a wharf? So much to learn and so much fun to be had.

I am 60 years of age and I still love fishing from a wharf. While there are lots of varieties of small fish that you may catch that are good to eat (sprats, piper and even spotties), once you get the knack of it all, you can upsize your gear and catch the larger eating fish that often have a habit of hanging out or turning up at your local wharf. I have witnessed large kingfish being landed off jetties, wharfs and piers on more than one occasion.

So have a go off the wharf — it's a cracking place to kick off what is sure to be a lifetime of adventures, camaraderie and hopefully stories about the one that didn't get away. Good luck out there.

Some things to keep in mind:

- Keep it simple when starting out fishing from a wharf. A lightweight rod and reel is the way to go. There are plenty of inexpensive choices at your local tackle store to get you started.

- Using smaller hooks will increase your hook-up rate.

- For bait, I'd go for squid as it's a tough bait that stays on your hook well, and can be cut into very small pieces to suit your hook size.

- 'Fish your feet' is a term you will often hear, which means fish the water close to you before casting further out. This means dropping the line directly below you first up. This will also give you time to understand how the reel works.

- Vary your depth. Start with your sinker on the sea floor, then try winding it up a metre or two. You will then find the sweet spot where the fish are located.

- When casting, always check behind you for hazards as you don't want to snag your hook on something — or, worse still, someone!

- Start with small casts then, as your confidence grows and you get the hang of it, you can start casting further out.

'The best way to catch a fish is to let him think he's escaping.' — Anonymous

- When you hook a fish, try to wind in slowly and steadily.

- Early morning and late afternoon, when the light is low, are usually more productive times.

- When you land a fish, handle it with a sea-soaked wet rag or towel, then gently remove the hook.

- If releasing, slip the fish as gently as possible back into the briny.

- If keeping the fish to eat or for bait, the most humane way to dispense of it is to use an iki spike on the head of the fish, killing it immediately.

KIT LIST
WHARF FISHING

- rods and reels
- tackle box
- hooks of various styles and sizes
- sabiki rigs
- sinkers of various sizes
- swivels
- monofilament leader of various weight strengths
- pliers
- snips
- knife
- small chopping board
- iki spike
- bucket
- bait
- old towel or rag
- chilly bin with salt ice
- sunscreen
- drinking water and snacks
- first-aid kit

FISHING
FROM A SMALL
BOAT OR
KAYAK

FISHING FROM A SMALL BOAT OR KAYAK

I think I'm probably correct when I say that most people fish from some sort of boat. The word 'boat' covers a lot of different things that float, including barges, jet skis, launches, ships, canoes, dinghies, kayaks and even paddle-boards. If it floats, people will probably have fished from it!

You don't need to have a big flash boat for your fishing adventures. Sure, if you're targeting marlin and tuna, then a large boat will get you out over the horizon for some big-game fishing. But a more modest boat still opens up an endless number of fishing spots inshore along the coastline. Indeed, my preferred way to fish is out of a kayak, usually soft-baiting in the shallows (often in water less than 10 metres deep).

When I go out in my 'fishing yak' I tend to follow a circuit, casting a couple of times here, moving on, then casting again a bit further on. I hardly ever catch a fish in the same spot twice.

The marine environment is always changing. While a few fish like to hang and make their home in a certain spot, most fish keep moving all the time, due to the current, the tide and where they can find food. It's just a matter of trying different spots as well as keeping one eye on the depth-sounder and fish-finder, and the other looking out for signs from Mother Nature.

The most important thing about heading out on the briny is returning safely. You must always respect the ocean and the weather, and safety is always your number one priority. When you're out on the water, conditions can change very, very quickly and not paying attention can end in tragedy. So take the time to make sure you're prepared, and you're sure to have a great day on the water.

'The best fishermen I know try not to make the same mistakes over and over again; instead, they strive to make new and interesting mistakes and to remember what they learned from them.'
— John Gierach

UNDERSTANDING THE RULES

Fishing out on the ocean or lake is a serious business, and there are more safety concerns and equipment required than if you were fishing from the beach, rocks or a wharf.

Coastguard New Zealand is an excellent resource for safe boating guidelines. I highly recommend downloading the Coastguard app and taking the time to look around their website (coastguard.nz). If you are 14 or over, I suggest checking out their Beginning Boating or Day Skipper courses (boatingeducation.org.nz/courses).

You could also download the NZ Fishing Rules app. This app is loaded with all the information you need about catch limits, rules for different regions, legal size of different species, how to handle and look after your precious catch, and loads more. The app has been put together by the Ministry of Primary Industries and it's a great resource for fishing in New Zealand.

There are two key rules to follow when you see another boat:

- When two boats are heading directly towards each other, both veer starboard (right) when passing.
- Powerboats must give way to boats under sail.

FISHING COMMANDMENTS

When you're fishing out on the open water, whether you're on a boat or in a kayak, there are some fishing 'commandments' that I recommend you run through every time before you go:

- Check the weather forecast before heading out.
- Let someone know where you are heading, and when you'll be back.
- Take at least one form of communication housed in a waterproof container. When I fish alone, I also carry a personal emergency locator beacon.
- Carry a first-aid kit.
- Pack extra warm clothes, no matter what the forecast.
- Always take kai and drinking water on any trips.

- Respect all fish, large or small.
- Before you leave the shore, decide how many fish you want to bring back with you to eat, then stick to the plan.
- Where possible always handle fish with a wet sea-soaked rag or towel, especially if you're releasing back into the briny.
- Use circle or barbless hooks if you are going to release the fish.
- Release fish gently back into the water. They are precious, and you want them to live. Even if they are small now, they may become the trophy-sized fish you catch later.
- Think about releasing large fish too. They are the breeders who ensure the species will continue to thrive.
- If you are going to keep a fish, iki it immediately.
- Always keep fish in a chilly bin, preferably with salt ice.
- Leave fish on ice for 24 hours before filleting.
- Try to use all the fish, not just the fillets.
- Don't freeze fish.
- Don't see the personal 'daily limit 'as a target.
- Bring rubbish back with you to dispose of properly, including any fishing rubbish like nylon and rusty hooks.
- Wash your rods and reels in fresh soapy water after each fishing session.

BOAT SPEAK

Aft — Behind or farthest back, often referred to as the back of the boat
Beam — The width of a vessel / boat from its widest point
Bow — The front of the boat
Fore — Forward, towards the front
Port — The lefthand side of the boat when facing the bow / red light
Starboard — The righthand side of the boat when facing the bow / green light
Stern — The back of the boat
Transom / Duckboard — The flat surface sticking out at right angles and attached to the stern of the boat
Windward — Facing the wind

KIT LIST
BOAT FISHING

- two forms of communication device, such as a UHF radio and a cell phone
- lifejackets for everyone on board, no exceptions
- rods and reels
- tackle box
- monofilament leader of various weight strengths
- hooks of various styles and sizes
- swivels
- split rings
- sinkers
- lures
- snips
- braid snips
- split-ring pliers
- knife
- bait board
- iki spike
- drogue
- anchor and chain
- long rope
- old towel or rags
- bait
- burley
- chilly bin with salt ice
- fish measure
- first-aid kit
- grab bag, which includes emergency locator beacon, flares, air horn, high-vis material, first-aid kit, whistle, waterproof torch
- jerry can with extra fuel
- sunscreen
- insect repellent
- extra warm clothes
- drinking water
- snacks and lunch

SURFCASTING

SURFCASTING

Surfcasting from a beach or off the rocks in an estuary or river mouth is such a fun way to fish. Even though New Zealand is a small country, our vast coastline means there are many incredible locations where you can cast a line from the shore.

I love all methods of fishing, and surfcasting is no exception. While I do fish from the beach at times, my favourite way to fish from the land is from a rocky outcrop, surrounded by relatively deep water.

What's great about surfcasting?

- The first obvious benefit is that you don't need a boat, which means you can be pretty light on your feet when it comes to what gear you need to get started.

- Another bonus is that most surfcasting rods and set-ups can be used in multiple situations, whether you're fishing from the sand or from a rocky headland.

- While it's unlikely that you'll be able to target deep-water species like marlin or hāpuka from the shore, there's still a wide variety of inshore fish to catch, and you can find plenty of opportunities to battle XXL fish like super-large snapper and kingfish. These big old fish are the species' best breeding stock, and when you catch and release them in shallow water their mortality rate is very low as they haven't been pulled up from the depths.

- And lastly, many fishing spots can only be accessed by casting from the shore.

Many people love fishing from the beach as it is often a pretty relaxed affair, with the rod placed securely in a rod-holder while the angler is parked up on deck chair, keeping a lazy eye on the tip of the rod for bites. However, while it's a pretty laid-back way to fish, you do need a good strong cast and a relatively long rod to hurl your line over the breaking waves, even if there is just a little swell running.

The old saying that 'the harder it is to get somewhere, the better the location' certainly works when it comes to finding spots that don't get fished often, and it is usually worth the effort. With a huge amount of coastline only able to be accessed through private land, having permission to fish from areas that don't get a lot of fishing pressure is pure gold.

Don't let this put you off — you may be surprised how often you can access these spots with a phone call first or just by fronting up, knocking on a door and politely asking permission to cross someone's farmland to the coast. A koha as a thankyou will often seal the deal and get you access, often for a lifetime. Just don't forget to close the gate!

Scrambling down a hill with a mate or two to fish off a rocky ledge dropping into deep water is exciting stuff. With all the kelp and seaweed present, these sorts of spots offer up some of the most exciting and excellent fishing opportunities, as they are environments where fish like to live.

When heading out for the day, give yourself plenty of time to plan and think through all the opportunities that may present themselves at these out-of-the-way spots. Most rods these days break down into two or three pieces, so see if you can pack a few rods and reels that offer up different combinations for different fishing opportunities.

While most folk fish with bait, having options to cast a lure as well will cover most situations. Use stick baits for kingies, and soft baits and hard lures for many other species.

BURLEY

Taking burley along with you will seriously up your chances of having a successful day. Essentially, burley is a frozen block of mashed-up fish scraps and the like. Some people create their own concoctions, but it's a messy job, so most places that sell regular fishing bait also sell 'burley bombs'. I find that burley bombs made with oilier fish such as salmon, sardines, etc work best, because when the natural oil of the fish leaches out you can literally see the burley trail from the oily slick visible on top of the water.

Once you've found the spot where you want to fish, the first job is to get the burley into the water. Either remove it from its plastic wrapper or cut holes in the wrapper before placing it in a designated burley container or, as I do, slip it into an onion sack. Add a little weight like a small rock to the sack, tie the top of the sack securely, then attach a length of rope to the top with the other end tied to the shore.

Place the burley sack in the area where you'd like to fish. The sloshing around and slow thawing of the burley in the water creates a trail of fishy goodness that attracts fish to the spot.

Small bait fish are usually the first to show up, followed by young fish from the species you are targeting, such as small snapper, kahawai and sprats. The larger (and wiser) fish most often turn up later and typically hang back as they are a bit more timid and wary.

SETTING UP FOR THE DAY

Once the burley is in the water, it's time to organise your day camp.

If you're fishing from the rocks, get familiar with the nooks and crannies of the ledge you are fishing from. It pays to observe the swell too. Where is it breaking? Where is an ideal spot to land a hooked fish? If it's low tide now, what will your environment be like once the tide turns and starts to come in? That little gut that you easily stepped over may be a completely different story at high tide.

Remember, especially if there is a bit of a swell running, never turn your back on the sea. Rogue waves can come out of nowhere, so it's a 'safety first' situation!

Fishing from the rocks in the intertidal zone — the area between high tide and low tide — is a spectacular experience. There is so much nature to take in. The coastal vegetation, the bird life, the surf and waves drifting in and out, not to mention the fish you encounter. Big 'rays' coming up the burly trail, kingfish smashing through bait fish only metres from you, large schools of kahawai or trevally eating small krill off the surface . . . It really is a fantastic way to fish. Every outing is different to the one before, but one thing is for certain: every trip will always be a big adventure.

'Fishing is not just about catching fish; it's about understanding the delicate balance of nature.'
— Aldo Leopold

KIT LIST
SURFCASTING

- surfcasting rod and reel
- surfcasting rod holder
- fishing line: monofilament leader of various weight strengths
- tackle box
- hooks of various sizes and styles
- swivels and split rings for your fishing rod
- breakaway sinkers of various weights
- pliers
- snips
- iki spike
- cotton
- knife
- chopping board
- old towel or rag
- bait, a couple of options (squid, pilchard, mussels, etc)
- burley
- foldaway deck chairs
- backpack with sunscreen, first-aid kit, insect repellent, beanie, jersey, water bottle, snacks and lunch
- chilly bin with salt ice

SAFETY

When fishing from the beach or rocks, keep these important things in mind:

- Let someone know where you are fishing and what time you expect to be home.
- Always have a mate, preferably an adult, with you when fishing from the shore around deep water.
- Always carry a first-aid kit.
- Pack lots of fresh water to drink and kai to eat.
- Wear suitable footwear for your surfcasting situation. Jandals on the beach are fine, but they are hopeless on the rocks.
- If you're fishing from the rocks, make sure you wear a lifejacket. There's always a possibility that you could fall into the water or be swept away by a rogue wave.
- Never turn your back on the sea. Rogue waves can and do come out of nowhere.

Always take your rubbish home with you. Plastic bags that house burley, bits of nylon and your general rubbish have no place in these pristine environments.

ON THE
FLY

ON THE FLY

While I love all fishing, fly fishing is probably my favourite. It is technically a bit more challenging, but like all types of fishing, the more you do it, the better you get. I have been fly fishing for nearly 40 years, and I am still learning every time I venture out.

What is fly fishing? It's a fishing technique that uses an artificial fly instead of bait to catch a fish. While you can fly fish in many situations, both fresh water and salt water, and for all sorts of fish, I think most fly fishing is performed walking up a river, a spring creek, on the edge of a lake or in a river mouth.

Fly fishers are a passionate bunch — there's something about the challenge of fooling a fish into thinking that the fly on the end of your line is a tasty insect or small fish!

I find the camaraderie from fly fishing hard to beat — I remember one particular day wandering up a river in the South Island in the middle of summer with my brother Jeremy and great mate Matto with just one fly rod between the three of us. Two of us would act as spotters, calling where a fish was positioned: 'See the kānuka bush with its branch in the water? The fish is a metre off the bank and half a rod-length upstream.' Whoever's turn it was with the rod got to cast. Then we'd carry on upstream, changing positions. It was such a fun way to fish, with everyone having a part to play, and tonnes of banter and hilarity thrown in for good measure.

THE JOY OF FLY FISHING

I think people get hooked on fly fishing (no pun intended) because of the joy in casting and mending, as well as a bunch of other reasons:

- Firstly, your body is in constant movement. Casting takes concentration; your mind is working hard while your arm goes back and forth, looking to land the fly in an exact spot.

- There are different types of fly fishing to master within the sport itself. When nymphing (see page 102), use an indicator that floats on top of the water; when it dips, you strike immediately. With a dry fly, you pause for a moment and strike when the fish turns back down into the water column. When fishing 'down and across' using a wet fly, the fish essentially hooks itself.

- The gear itself is quite different to the gear you typically use in saltwater situations. For instance, the rods are a lot longer because this helps to cast the flies, which are very light. The rods are often a lot lighter than saltwater rods.

- The terminal tackle is also quite different to what you use when fishing the briny. It is super-light gear, with very small hooks, which makes fighting and ultimately landing a trout or similar extremely rewarding. However, be prepared — the trout often wins the battle!

- You don't use bait or burley. There is something really satisfying about fooling a fish through sight only. This is where the term 'matching the hatch' comes from, meaning you need to understand what is happening in nature and what the fish are eating, then tie on an imitation of that insect or minnow to ultimately fool the fish.

- Tying your own flies rather than using store-bought is also very satisfying and adds another layer of reward and dimension to the sport. Like learning to cast, it takes plenty of practice to tie a decent foolproof pattern. However, there are a few nymphs and wet fly patterns that are relatively easy to learn to tie first up, and then it is onwards and upwards from there.

There's so much to learn about fly fishing — I hope this introduction has made you keen to give it a go. If you get the opportunity to learn the first few basic steps, I doubt you'll look back, and you also will never look at a river, stream or backwater in the same way again.

FLY-FISHING TECHNIQUES

There are many different fly-fishing styles in use around the world. Here in New Zealand, there are four techniques that we traditionally use: nymphing, dry fly, wet fly / streamer and dry dropper.

Nymphing

Nymphing is when you are fishing weighted flies below the surface, typically bouncing them along the bottom of the stream. The nymphs represent aquatic insects, larvae and worms.

Dry fly

Dry fly is fishing using an imitation of an insect that has either hatched after the nymph stage of the life cycle and is floating on the water surface, or an insect that has landed on the surface of the water.

Wet fly / streamer

Wet fly or fishing a streamer fly is imitating a whitebait smelt or small fish like a cockabully. The fly is often tied with a feather, and is cast across the stream then swung through the current as it is slowly retrieved.

Dry dropper

Dry dropper is where you are fishing a large enough dry fly to stay on the surface, with a small nymph sitting around a foot underneath the surface.

All four techniques have their time and place, and it pays to learn them all. However, most fly fishers would agree that whatever technique you choose, sight-fishing for trout in crystal-clear water with a dry fly and watching the fish move some distance to take your offering is absolutely 'heart in your mouth' stuff, forging yet another a memory you will never forget.

LEARNING TO CAST

When you mention 'fly fishing', the image that comes into most people's mind is of a graceful cast where the long line forms a beautiful loop behind the angler the moment before it starts its trajectory forward. To watch an experienced, skilled fly fisher cast is absolutely mesmerising.

Casting is all about rhythm, timing and control of your line. To seasoned fly fishers, it almost becomes second nature; however, you can be sure even the best casters of a fly line are humbled most days with awkward moments when a cast gets away on them, or the hook ends up in a shrub or round a branch behind them.

You don't need to be over water to learn to cast. Just find a good-sized patch of lawn where you can practise. Parks are a perfect spot. You will be surprised how quickly you

'The act of fishing takes us to the hidden corners of the world, revealing the beauty that lies beneath the surface.'
— James Prosek

can pick it up. And when you do, like swinging a golf club, hitting a tennis ball or shooting a hoop, it's all about the timing. It's a wonderful feeling when you start to nail a few casts, and you know what? It only gets better the more you practise — no surprises there!

The great thing is that you can learn to cast relatively quickly. You will need someone experienced to give you your first lesson and the key points to think about as the line shoots forward and back past your head at a decent skip.

Here are some basic steps to follow:

1. Grip the rod. With your shoulders square, hold the rod with your thumb on top and your fingers wrapped around the handle. Keep a firm but relaxed grip.

2. Start with line out. Pull out about 3–5 metres of line from the reel. Let it lie on the ground or water in front of you.

3. Position the rod. Hold the rod tip low. Your wrist should be straight.

4. The back cast. Smoothly and swiftly lift the rod behind you, letting the line follow. Pause briefly to let the line extend behind you.

5. The forward cast. Move the rod forward in a quick, controlled motion. The line will follow, unfurling in front of you. Stop with the tip of the rod high.

6. Release the line. As the line extends forward, release more line from your hand. This will help the line reach further.

7. Stop the rod. As the line is about to land, lower the rod tip. This helps the line lay out smoothly on the water.

Probably the next most important thing to learn is 'mending', which is where you move or lift your fly line gently off the water either up or downstream, to eliminate the drag on the flies or nymphs that you are fishing. Fish, especially trout, are intelligent creatures and no matter how well your fly matches the insect it is mimicking, if it's not flowing at the same rate as the current, the fish won't touch it.

THE GEAR

Rods

Similar to all fishing rods, fly rods come in a variety of lengths and weights, which gives the angler options around the environment they are fishing in and the size of the species they are targeting. Heavier rods with a higher line weight offer more power and are better for casting larger and heavier nymphs and flies. They also give you more distance over larger expanses of water, and make it easier to cast when there is wind about. Lighter rods with lighter lines are designed for fishing smaller waters like a spring creek where a more delicate, stealthy cast is required.

Unlike most other forms of fishing where you cast a heavy(ish) terminal tackle, with fly fishing you are essentially casting the weight of the fly line itself. If you are new to the sport it probably pays to start off with a medium-weight rod: a 2.7 metre long, 6 or 7 weight rod would be ideal. Then if you really get into it, you can buy heavier and lighter rods to suit your requirements.

Like most kit in life, there is a huge range in price, mostly due to the material the rod is made of. You don't need to get carried away, especially when you are learning: a more expensive rod and reel might look good but won't make you a better angler.

Fly reels

Once you have selected your fly rod, it is important to purchase a fly reel and line that suits the weight of the rod. It's all about the balance of the set-up. So, if you have purchased a 7 weight rod, you'll need a reel that will carry a 7 weight line.

Floating lines

These lines are specifically designed for fly fishing, and are the most common fly lines especially when freshwater fishing. With a relatively wide girth, the coating of the floating line gives it the buoyancy to float on top of the water and also helps keep it airborne when casting.

Floating lines are always tapered. There are weight forward (WF) lines which makes it easier to cast, especially if there is a breeze to contend with, and double taper (DT) where the weight is situated in the middle of the floating line to help the angler when casting in a

very delicate presentation. The weight of the line you are using should match the weight of the fly rod it is attached to.

To the floating line you then tie on a long leader of fluoro or mono, usually around a rod length, then attach whatever fly-fishing terminal tackle you are using.

Sinking lines

Sinking lines are a more dense type of fly-fishing line that sinks when cast. There are slow, intermediate and fast sinking lines which you choose to match the depth and the current of river you are fishing, in order to present your fly at the depth that the fish are situated. Sinking lines are mainly used for wet line fishing, where the chosen fly is usually a streamer imitating a small smelt or minnow.

Shooting heads

This is a shorter version of a weighted sinking line that has a heavy head, making it relatively easy to cast long distances. It is only a couple of metres long. They sink very quickly, getting the fly down to the fish zone rapidly and efficiently and are preferred these days to the traditional sinking line. Easy to cast, they shoot out at speed and the angler can achieve good distance when presenting the fly.

'A fisherman's skill is born from moments of stillness and patterns of movement.'
— Bryant McGill

Leaders

The leader is made of nylon or fluorocarbon tied directly to the fly line, with your fly or nymph positioned at the end. There are different strengths, so you normally carry a range, depending on things like the size of the fish you are targeting or the water environment you are fishing.

Tapered leaders

This is another type of leader, mostly used when dry-fly fishing. As the name suggests, it is tapered — it's stronger and thicker at the end connected to the fly line and then thinner at the other end, which helps when casting and turning over the fly when you let the cast go.

Tippets

The tippet is the end of the fly-fishing leader. It's nylon or fluorocarbon, is fine in diameter and is used to extend the leader, which will change the breaking strength.

Fly box
This holds all your flies, nymphs and streamers. Most anglers will have their favourite patterns and in several different sizes too. The fly box holds each fly individually and in an orderly manner, which looks after them and helps with selection.

Snips or scissors
Carried by the angler to snip or cut the 'tags' of nylon or fluorocarbon that are left after a knot has been tied.

Indicators
An indicator is a floating device that helps you see when a fish has eaten your fly. They are mainly used when fishing nymph flies. The indicator is typically made of yarn or another floating material, and is either tied near the top of the leader or where the leader is connected to the floating fly line. It signals to the angler, by moving or submerging, that a fish has taken the nymph, in which case you strike immediately. Unfortunately it can also indicate that you have hooked the bottom or a sunken log.

Floatant
Floatant is a liquid or powder applied to the indicator and dry flies to help them stay afloat when sitting on top of the water. Used also to help indicators float.

'In fishing, as in life, opportunity is often a matter of being in the right place at the right time.'
— Larry Koller

Forceps
Forceps are used to help remove the hook from a caught fish.

Nets
A portable net will usually have a clip so you can attach it to your belt or the back of your fishing vest.

Vests and kit bags
An 'old school' fly fishing vest is probably still the most common piece of kit to hold all the bits and bobs you need when fly fishing. There are, however, also quite a few new other nifty bags on the market, with belts to go around your waist or across your chest. Choose whatever you feel works best for you.

Waders
There are a couple of options here. Most people these days wear light

breathable waders made of Gore-Tex. However, if you fly fish in winter some prefer the heavier neoprene version with built-in rubber boots.

FLY BOX

History tells us that the first person to write about his fishing adventures was a Roman chap called Claudius Aelianus, who apparently tied a piece of red wool and a couple of feathers to a hook in Macedonia in 200AD. However the modern form of fly fishing has been attributed to a guy called Charles Cotton, who was a poet and English aristocrat who co-wrote and published a book called *The Compleat Angler* in 1676. Yes, that's how they spelled the word 'complete' back then. So fly fishing has been around for centuries.

I presume the term 'match the hatch' was coined sometime way back then too. It explains in just three simple words what fly fishing is all about. The angler is simply observing nature at that moment in time, working out exactly what invertebrate, flying bug or aquatic insect has hatched and is on offer for the fish's breakfast, lunch or dinner. They then tie an imitation of that mayfly, beetle, midge, mite or spider on their line.

The many distinctly different insects which are food for the fish you're targeting are the inspiration for the hundreds of assorted flies you could tie.

Below are an assortment of the flies I think most fly fishers would have in their fly boxes, simply because they are tried and true and have delivered the goods on many occasions. It will always be a matter for discussion, which is part of the fun of it all.

It pays to have different sizes and weights of the same pattern, as it is all about 'matching the hatch' on the day.

Nymphs
Hare and Coppers, Pheasant Tail, Prince Nymph, Stoneflies (various patterns), Caddis (various colours), Blood Worm, Glow Bug, Willow Grub, Pheasant Tail Flashback, Copper Johnny

Dry flies
Parachute Adams, Kakahi Queen, Humpies, Royal Wolf, Blow Fly, Cicada, Dad's Favourite, Caddis Emerger, Green Beetle, Black Gnat

Streamers / wet flies
Smelt Fly, Parson's Glory, Woolly Bugger (various colours), Rabbit Fly (various colours), Grey Ghost, Scotch Poacher, Booby Fly (various colours), Hamil's Killer, Doll Fly (various colours), Mrs Simpson, Red Setter

KIT LIST
FLY FISHING

- fly fishing vest
- waders
- wading belt
- wading boots
- Polaroid dark glasses
- hat
- backpack with a beanie, jersey, rain jacket, sunscreen, insect repellent, first-aid kit, water bottle, snacks / lunch
- phone / personal locator beacon
- fly rod
- reel
- fly box with dry flies, nymphs, streamers
- split-shot sinkers
- indicators
- fluorocarbon tippet with multiple breaking strain options
- tapered leaders
- clippers
- forceps
- pocket knife
- floatant
- landing net

YOU'VE CAUGHT A FISH!
NOW WHAT?

YOU'VE CAUGHT A FISH! NOW WHAT?

Catching a fish is always a buzz. First there is the anticipation, then you feel the bite and then that magical feeling of lifting your rod and feeling the weight come on. You feel the first pull of the fish, giving an early indication of its size as the line peels off your reel and you watch your rod bend towards the water.

Whether you are experiencing this for the first time or you are a seasoned pro, the feeling of hooking, fighting and ultimately landing a fish never ever gets old.

There are a few things to think about once you have landed a fish or two to take home and eat. While the catching is definitely high-octane stuff, there's nearly as much enjoyment to be had after you have caught and decided to keep them.

'If I fished only to capture fish, my fishing trips would have ended long ago.'
— Zane Grey

Fish are precious and delicate creatures, and it is super important to treat them with respect. If you're not going to be eating the fish or using it for bait, unhook it as quickly as possible and carefully slip it back

into the water to live another day. If you are keeping the fish, make sure you end its life humanely.

If you look after your catch by adhering to the points below, you will be rewarded with the best eating and tasting fish imaginable.

No matter whether you are fishing off a wharf, in a boat or off the rocks, one of the most important bits of kit that you should always carry is an old towel or tea-towel. Soak it in salt water, ready and at hand for all the fish you catch, whether you are keeping them or releasing them.

The wet towel makes handling a feisty fish much easier, as fish are strong and very slippery. It also helps to protect you from sharp spikes and fins. When you drape the wet towel over the fish's head, it'll calm down and be way easier to handle.

If you have decided to keep the fish lay it flat, secure on a solid surface with the wet towel over its eyes. If the fish is hooked in the side of the mouth it should be reasonably easy to dislodge the hook. Hold the fish still, grip the shank and the eye of the hook firmly and twist it out, essentially reversing the way the hook was lodged. Place the hook back on the rod so it's not dangling about while you deal with the next step in the process.

Now it's time to dispatch the fish as quickly and as humanely as possible. There are a couple of ways to do this:

- While holding the fish securely, take a wooden mallet or club and knock the fish on the head with two sharp blows.

- Or, drive a sharp spike into the fish's brain on the side of its head. This is a Japanese method called 'iki jime', which kills the fish instantly. This takes a little practice, but once you get the hang of it it's relatively simple. You will learn the spot to penetrate with the spike, as the fish goes limp immediately. It's also proven to minimise the stress of the fish and helps maximise the eating quality of the fish.

Next, chill your fish down as quickly as possible. Before you head out, it's best to make an ice slurry (two parts ice and one part water) in a chilly bin. Saltwater ice is preferable to freshwater ice as it lasts quite a bit longer, but you can make it with either type of ice. Place the fish in the ice slurry to bring down its core temperature. Once it's chilled through, place it in another chilly bin and toss over some ice. Keep the lid closed. This will keep the fish in tip-top condition.

I know this sounds like a bit of a faff, but trust me, if you look after your catch in this way, you will absolutely be rewarded when you come to eat the fish.

I like to keep my fish on ice for at least 12 hours before filleting them. This gives time for the fillets to firm up and makes the filleting process easier and more enjoyable.

HOW TO FILLET A FISH

Here is the equipment you'll need for filleting fish:

- scaler
- sharp filleting knife
- kitchen snips/scissors
- chopping board
- clean dry cloth or towel
- bucket.

'Scaling a fish' is the process of removing the scales from the fish while leaving the skin on and intact. I always scale my fish before filleting, as it makes filleting a lot easier and more enjoyable. If possible I also like to scale my fish standing in the sea, as scales go everywhere. A fish scaler makes removing the scales quick and easy. There are plenty of styles of fish scalers out there, and they are inexpensive. If you don't have access to a scaler, use something like a dessert spoon. To scale, you simply pull the scaler across the scales from the tail to the head, turning the fish as you go.

Now it's time to get a bit messy. When learning to fillet a fish, always have an experienced adult supervising you. To fillet a fish:

1. Make sure your fish is dry, so it lays securely on your chopping board and use a sharp knife, preferably a knife designed to fillet fish.

2. To remove the guts, run the knife from the poo hole back to the head. Open the cavity and grab the innards with your hand, then pull them through the opening and discard.

3. Rinse the cavity clean — if you can use salt water, all the better.

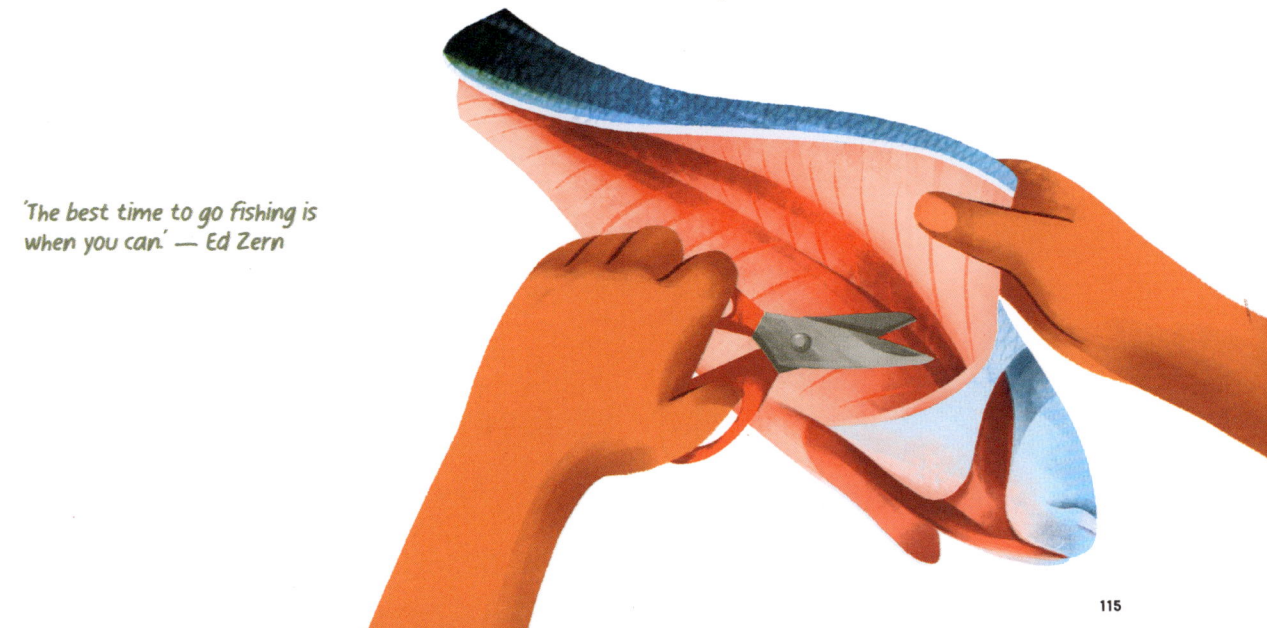

4. To remove the head of the fish, on an angle cut down each side of the pectoral fin between the head and the fillets. Use the heel of the knife or the kitchen snips to cut through the backbone, removing the head.

5. If keeping the fish wings (a great idea on a larger fish), lay the head of the fish flat and use the knife to cut out the gills and discard. Cut the triangles that run from the belly up to the top of the head, with the pectoral fin positioned in the centre of both. Check for any pesky scales still attached and remove and discard the fins using the kitchen snips.

6. Make sure the headless fish is dry and secure on the chopping board with its belly facing you. Run the knife through the skin along the length of the fish, from the head to the tail. As the fish fillet starts to appear, try to keep the blade of the

'The best time to go fishing is when you can.' — Ed Zern

knife gliding along the frame of the fish to eliminate wastage. Glide your knife over the backbone to capture the underside of the fillet. You will naturally hit the rib cage on both sides of the fish. This is where I use the snips to cut through both sides of the rib cage.

7. You now have two separate fillets. Lay a fillet skin-side down and remove the rib bone cavity with the knife. You will notice that there is one more line of bones, which we call the pin bones. Run your knife either side of the pin bones to where they finish, then lift them out and discard. Repeat with the other fillet.

Congrats, you now have two beautiful fillets, plus the head (gills removed), the frame and the trim from the filleting that can be used either to make a beautiful fish stock or as great bait for a craypot. I love to keep the skin on as it's delicious when cooked, kind of like fish crackling.

If you'd like to remove the skin, though, lay the fillet skin-side down and insert the knife about a centimetre from the end of the tail, between the fillet and the skin. Holding the tail of the fillet firmly, use a sawing motion to cut against (not through) the skin, pulling the skin towards you, until it has all come away.

Your precious fresh filleted fish is now ready for the frying pan, although if you have looked after and cared for the fish from the moment you landed it, it can keep for nearly a week in the fridge. To store the fillets, keep them clean, covered and dry. I lay them on a couple of sheets of paper towel, then check them every couple of days, as moisture will naturally be pulled from the fillets. Just pat the fillets dry, then discard the old paper towels. Lay the fillets on a fresh towel, cover and place back in the fridge. Don't be tempted to rinse them in fresh water, as this speeds up the ageing.

If you can keep all these best-practice points front of mind when looking after your catch, it will soon become a habit. You'll end up with fish that is delicious to eat and you will be paying the ultimate respect to these special fish that inhabit our coastline.

'In every species of fish I've angled for, it is the ones that have got away that thrill me the most, the ones that keep fresh in my memory. So I say it is good to lose fish. If we didn't, much of the thrill of angling would be gone.'
— Ray Bergman

COOKING UP YOUR CATCH

COOKING UP YOUR CATCH

I think cooking fish that you have caught yourself is one of life's real joys. It's why so many people love to fish.

There is a huge sense of pride that comes when you've learnt how to catch a fish, and I feel the same way about preparing that fish to be eaten.

Sure, the adventure and anticipation of going fishing is a big part of the joy of fishing, and the battle that comes from hooking and landing a fish is always exciting. But I think there's also pleasure in honouring the fish by dispatching it humanely, icing it down, scaling, gutting and filleting it and finally cooking and serving the catch itself.

It takes a lifetime to become a whizz at all aspects of fishing. That is one of the reasons why we love to fish, as the learning curve really never ends.

Like with most of my cooking, when it comes to seafood I like to make food that can be shared, is relatively easy to prepare, and where the fish is always the hero of the dish.

I hope you give a few of the following recipes a crack. Cooking is always more fun when there's two of you in the kitchen, so get Mum or Dad or another adult to help you with any tricky bits.

Lastly, when serving the fish to the folks around the table, always regale them with tall tales of the epic battle you fought with the fish they are about to enjoy. As that old saying goes, 'Don't let the truth get in the way of a good story!'

HOW TO COOK THE PERFECT FISH FILLET

While I love all the recipes that follow, I also enjoy nothing more than a fresh piece of fish, seasoned with salt and fresh black pepper, then simply cooked in a pan with a little oil, finished with a lick of butter and a squeeze of lemon or lime juice. Timeless, and so simple and so delicious.

Tips for cooking fresh fish:

- The thicker the fillet, the longer it will take to cook.
- Oily fish such as kahawai, trevally and kingfish tend to dry out when cooked more than fillets of non-oily white fish.
- The golden rule is to always err on the side of slightly undercooking fish fillets, as they will continue to cook a little once removed from the pan. You can always cook them a little more if needed, but there is no going back if you have overcooked a piece of fish.
- You must cook whole fish all the way through, so the fish pulls away from the bones with ease. Cooking on the bone also helps to keep the fillet moist.
- Try cooking fish fillets scaled but with the skin on. The skin ends up as a crispy fish crackling. There is also a micro-layer of fat between the skin and the fillet which again helps to keep the fillet moist.
- Always heat your pan up to at least medium-high heat. I like to use a cast-iron skillet to cook my fish — it's the original non-stick pan, and it retains its heat when the fish is added to the pan.
- For best results, bring the raw fillets up to room temperature before cooking.

COOKING DIFFERENT VARIETIES OF FISH

I often find myself harping on about eating the 'other' fish to anyone who will listen. So many people try to only catch the popular varieties of fish when they head out to catch a feed. I get it — snapper, blue cod, tarakihi and gurnard are all delicious to eat. But there are so many other types of fish that taste just as good!

The challenge is learning about different ways to cook and serve certain varieties. For instance, many people think that kahawai are only good for smoking. Codswallop! Kahawai can be prepared and cooked in nearly every eating situation you can possibly think of: raw (sashimi), ceviche, smoked, grilled, roasted whole, deep-fried in batter . . .

You just need to keep a few things in mind:

- If it is a small-flaked fish, chances are it has a more delicate and subtle taste. Great for cooking, eg pan-fried, poached or crumbed.

  Examples: gurnard, tarakihi, blue cod, snapper, butterfish, John Dory

- Larger-flaked fish can handle more robust styles of preparation and cooking. Think pan-fried, in stews and chowders, barbecued, chargrilled, battered and deep-fried, and crumbed.

  Examples: hāpuka, warehou, monkfish, bluenose, blue moki, pōrae

- Some varieties of fish are described as being 'oily' in texture. Oily fish are generally wonderful to sashimi or marinate. The main thing to watch when cooking oily fish is not to overcook them. In fact, if oily fish are still a little raw or opaque in the centre, that's perfect.

  Examples: salmon, tuna, kingfish, kahawai, grey mullet, mackerel, trevally

- In the past, fishers have generally targeted the larger fish while ignoring the smaller varieties, because they think the smaller varieties are bait fish. Sure, smaller fish do make great bait, but they also reward you in the eating stakes. This style of eating requires you to slow down a little and be patient, because we often cook small fish whole. This means they stand up to more rigorous cooking styles, such as barbecuing, sautéing, chargrilling and oven roasting.

  Examples: yellow-eyed mullet, pilchards, piper / garfish, jack mackerel

'DEPOT' FISH SLIDERS
WITH PRESERVED LEMON MAYO AND WATERCRESS

For better or worse, this is my most popular recipe in my 40-odd years as a chef. I have calculated we've served over one million of these humble little fish burgers. Many would say the sliders are my signature dish — it's a little disconcerting that I'm going to be remembered for my take on a McDonald's Filet-O-Fish.

SERVES 6

STEP 1: PRESERVED LEMON MAYO

1 cup mayonnaise
3 tablespoons finely diced preserved lemon rind
2 tablespoons lemon juice
flaky sea salt & freshly ground black pepper

Place all the ingredients except the salt and pepper in a bowl. Whisk until combined, then season with salt and pepper. Refrigerate until required.

STEP 2: COOKING AND SERVING

800 g (1 lb 12 oz) fresh fish (whatever you prefer)
flaky sea salt & freshly ground black pepper
cooking oil
20 slider buns, split in half and buttered on both sides of each half-bun
preserved lemon mayo
watercress or similar leafy salad vegetable

Preheat the oven to 100°C (200°F).
    Heat up a skillet or flat-top barbecue to medium-high heat.
    Slice the fish into pieces about the same width as the slider buns. Season with salt and pepper.
    Add a little cooking oil to the skillet, then cook the fish pieces in batches, keeping them warm in the oven once they are cooked.
    Wipe down the skillet or barbeque flat-top, then caramelise both sides of both halves of each slider bun.
    Spread generous amounts of the preserved lemon mayo on both insides of the bun.
    Place a piece of fish on each bottom bun, add a couple of leaves of watercress then top with the lid of the bun.
    Serve immediately. They will be gone in a flash!

BEST FISH PIE EVER

Fish pie is comfort food personified. It is, without question, one of my favourite dishes to eat. You can riff with this recipe: use smoked fish, add some prawns, try some kina tongues, leave out the eggs, etc . . . I use kūmara as well as potato to add a little earthy sweetness to the pie.

The other great thing about fish pie is it's a great way to 'stretch the catch' to make the fish go further, if your luck has run out and the fish are proving tricky to find.

SERVES 6

STEP 1: FISH PIE FILLING

⅓ cup canola oil
1 cup finely diced onion
½ cup finely diced celery
½ cup finely diced carrot
2 cloves garlic, finely minced
1½ tablespoons finely minced fresh thyme
50 g (1¾ oz) butter
50 g (1¾ oz) all-purpose flour

4 cups milk
1 cup cream
flaky sea salt & freshly ground black pepper
2 lemons, zest and juice
hot sauce, a few drops to taste
1 kg (2 lb 4 oz) fresh white fish, cut into large pieces
2 cups frozen peas
3 eggs, hard-boiled and roughly chopped

Place a large saucepan on medium-high heat. Once hot, add the oil along with the onion, celery, carrot, garlic and fresh thyme. Stir to combine, then lower the heat to a simmer and cook the veges for about 20 minutes, stirring occasionally, until soft. Remove from the heat and set aside.

    For the white sauce, place another saucepan on medium-low heat. Add the butter and once melted add the flour. Stir to combine. Slowly add the milk and cream, whisking all the time until it is well mixed. Turn the heat down, then add the salt and pepper, lemon zest, lemon juice and hot sauce to taste.

    Cook the white sauce for 5 minutes or so, stirring to make sure there are no lumps, then pour the white sauce over the cooked veges. Stir to mix.

    Place the saucepan back on medium-low heat and bring back up to a simmer. Once the mixture is bubbling, with a wooden spoon stir in the chunks of fresh white fish. Cook for a minute or two, then remove the saucepan from the heat and stir in the frozen peas and chopped hard-boiled eggs.

    Pour the fish-pie mixture into an ovenproof dish. Let it cool, then refrigerate to help it set before topping with the kūmara and potato topping.

STEP 2: KŪMARA AND POTATO TOPPING

1 kg (2 lb 4 oz) kūmara, peeled and cut into large chunks
500 g (1 lb 2 oz) floury potatoes, peeled and cut into large chunks
50 g (1¾ oz) butter, diced into small cubes
1 cup cream
milk
flaky sea salt & freshly ground black pepper

Using separate saucepans, add the kūmara to one and the potato to the other and cover with cold water. Place on high heat, bring up to the boil, then turn down to a simmer. Once the kūmara have come to the boil, cook for approximately 10 minutes, until soft through. For the potatoes, check doneness using a fork after the potato has been boiling for 10 minutes.

Once the veges are cooked, remove each saucepan from the stove and drain the water. Add the potato to the kūmara, along with the butter and cream. Mash until smooth. If you want a softer, smoother mash, add a little milk. Season with salt and black pepper. While the mash is still warm, spread over the now-set fish-pie filling. Refrigerate until required.

STEP 3: CRUNCHY TOPPING

50 g (1¾ oz) butter, diced into small cubes
2 lemons, zest and juice
½ baguette (or similar bread), diced into small cubes
½ cup breadcrumbs

Melt the butter and add the zest and juice of the lemons. Place the chopped-up baguette in a bowl, then pour over the melted butter and toss through. Add the breadcrumbs.

Spread the topping evenly over the kūmara and potato mash on the top of the fish pie. Refrigerate or freeze until required.

STEP 4: COOKING AND SERVING

Defrost the fish pie if frozen. If refrigerated, bring the fish pie out of the fridge an hour before placing in the oven.

Preheat the oven to 160°C (315°F).

Place the fish pie in the centre of the oven. Cook for 30 to 40 minutes, until heated through and the topping is crisp and golden. A simple green salad and some fresh bread for mopping up the sauce make perfect accompaniments.

FISH HEAD AND BACON CHOWDER

I believe most New Zealand fishers (myself included) have been guilty of wasting a lot of our catch in the past. We would whip the fillets off and then discard the rest of the frame, or it would end up in a crayfish pot. Things are definitely changing in this department as we are starting to really understand that fish numbers are finite.

The following recipe uses parts of the fish that used to be thrown away. Fish heads have incredible flavour, so making a stock out of them and turning it into a creamy chowder is a meal to dream of!

SERVES 6 (WITH SOME FOR SECONDS)

STEP 1: FISH HEAD STOCK

2 or 3 fish heads (gills removed) and frames
2 onions, roughly chopped
2 carrots, roughly chopped
2 or 3 celery sticks, roughly chopped
½ leek, roughly chopped
3 cloves garlic, roughly chopped

handful chopped parsley
3 bay leaves
12 peppercorns
2 cups white wine
4 to 5 litres cold water

I like to split my fish heads open with a cleaver or heavy-duty kitchen scissors. It's optional, but I'm sure it pumps up the flavour.

Take a large saucepan, and add all the ingredients except the cold water. Place the saucepan on medium-high heat, and place a lid on top for about 10 minutes.

Remove the lid, and pour in the cold water. Turn the heat up to high. Once the stock is boiling, turn it down to a simmer. Let it simmer away for an hour or more. Strain off all the solids, and retain the fish stock.

Taste the stock. There should be great flavour, but if you want to intensify it a bit more place the stock back on the heat and reduce it until you are happy with how it tastes.

STEP 2: CHOWDER

⅓ cup canola oil
250 g (9 oz) bacon, diced into small cubes
2 onions, diced into small cubes
2 carrots, diced into small cubes
2 stalks celery, diced into small cubes
1 leek, diced into small cubes
3 garlic cloves, minced finely

120 g (4¼ oz) butter, diced
120 g (4¼ oz) all-purpose flour
12 cups fish stock
1½ cups cream
1 lemon, zest and juice
hot sauce, to taste
flaky sea salt & freshly ground black pepper

Place a large saucepan on medium heat. Once hot, add the oil followed by the bacon. Cook over medium heat for 5 to 10 minutes until crisp and the fat has rendered and gone clear.

Add the chopped onion, carrot, celery, leek and garlic. Turn the heat down to low, and cook the veges for 20 to 30 minutes, stirring occasionally, until they are soft.

While the veges are cooking, take another large saucepan and place on medium-high heat. Add the butter and let it melt, then add the flour and whisk until combined.

Add the fish stock a few ladles at a time, whisking continuously. Continue until you are happy with the consistency of the chowder. I like my chowder to be silky smooth with plenty of body, but not too thick.

Add the cream, lemon zest and lemon juice, and some hot sauce to your liking. Taste, then adjust the seasoning with salt and pepper.

Add the cooked veges and bacon to the liquid. Stir through, then cool and refrigerate until required.

STEP 3: COOKING AND SERVING

chowder base
1 kg (2 lb 4 oz) seafood of your choice (such as white fish, smoked fish, mussels or prawns)
fresh Italian parsley, finely chopped
fresh dill, finely diced

Heat the chowder over medium-low heat, stirring occasionally. Once simmering, add the seafood to cook (about 5 minutes). Finally, stir in the fresh herbs just prior to serving.

Serve in hot bowls with a big chunk of garlic bread on the side. Nothing could be more Kiwi. Yum!

LUCKY CHOCOLATE FISH SLICE

There's nothing better than a slice of sweet goodness when you are out on the ocean or walking up a stream. Eating outdoors seems to amplify the flavour of whatever you're eating. It also lifts your spirits and breaks the monotony if the fish aren't biting. This slice is super fun to make, as it's a no-bake affair. I have made this for a couple of fishing trips recently, and both times I had a PB (personal best) — hence the name 'Lucky'!

MAKES 18 PIECES

STEP 1: SLICE

100 g (3½ oz) butter, roughly chopped
395 g (14 oz) sweetened condensed milk
150 g (5½ oz) dark chocolate, broken into pieces
250 g (9 oz) vanilla wine biscuits or similar
½ cup desiccated coconut
½ cup currants
2 tablespoons cocoa
18 mini chocolate fish

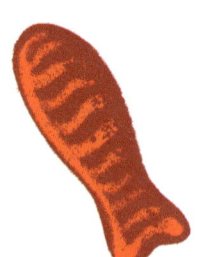

Place a saucepan on low heat. Add the butter, condensed milk and dark chocolate. Let the butter and chocolate melt, then stir to combine.

In a bowl, crush the vanilla wine biscuits to a rough-cut crumb, then add the coconut, currants and cocoa. Mix.

Pour the melted chocolate over the crushed biscuits and mix everything together.

Line a slice tin with baking paper. Place the mixture in the lined tin, then pat down until evenly spread. Gently press the mini chocolate fish into the warm mixture.

STEP 2: CHOCOLATE ICING

300 g (10½ oz) dark chocolate, broken into pieces
2 tablespoons vegetable oil or coconut oil

Place a saucepan on medium heat with some boiling water in the bottom. Place a stainless steel bowl on top of the saucepan. Add the chocolate and oil to the bowl and melt until combined.

Once the chocolate is shiny and smooth, pour over the slice, moving the tin around so all the fish are covered.

Chill, then slice into 18 pieces with a fish in the middle of each. Store in an airtight container or cake tin.

SASHIMI
WITH SOY SYRUP, KEWPIE AND WASABI PEAS

This is a crazy-good and super-easy recipe, and I swear everyone loves it. It's been on the Depot menu for a few years now, and many customers start their dining experience with this dish, followed by fish sliders. The only thing you have to do is combine and reduce two ingredients (soy sauce and sugar), and the other ingredients are simply store-bought — except for the fish, of course, which should be in pristine condition and as fresh as possible. This dish is a favourite for a number of reasons: it's fresh, salty, sweet, has a little heat and its texture works brilliantly.

SERVES 6

STEP 1: SOY SYRUP

1 cup soy sauce
1 cup sugar

Place a small saucer or plate in the fridge.

Place a saucepan on medium-high heat, and add the soy sauce and sugar. Bring to a simmer and reduce slightly for about 10 minutes to create a thick but still runny syrup.

The liquid will always be runnier when it's hot, so that's where the cold saucer comes in. With a spoon, place a couple of drops on the cold saucer to see how reduced it is. Most people over-reduce the syrup. When it's the right consistency, remove from the heat and store in a jar. The syrup can be stored at room temperature or refrigerated.

STEP 2: PLATING AND SERVING

600 g (1 lb 5 oz) super-fresh fish
Kewpie mayonnaise
soy syrup
⅓ cup roughly crushed wasabi peas
micro basil or finely chopped fresh basil

Slice the fish thinly with a sharp knife. Arrange on a platter. Add a drop of mayo on each piece. Drizzle over a little of the soy syrup, scatter over the crushed wasabi peas and finish with the basil. Serve immediately.

MUSSEL AND KŪMARA FRITTERS
WITH TARTARE SAUCE

Who doesn't like a fritter? For this recipe I have used mussels and kūmara, which feels very Aotearoa to me, but by all means play around with different main ingredients. Keep the rest of the batter the same. Fritters also are really useful when you need to stretch the catch or, for that matter, the cash!

MAKES 12 LARGE FRITTERS OR 24 SMALL FRITTERS

STEP 1: TARTARE SAUCE

1 cup mayonnaise
¼ cup wholegrain mustard
1 green capsicum, finely diced
⅓ cup finely diced red onion
⅓ cup finely diced gherkin
¼ cup roughly chopped capers
1 lemon, zest and juice
⅓ cup finely chopped parsley
flaky sea salt & freshly ground black pepper

Place all the ingredients except the salt and pepper in a bowl. Mix together, taste, then season accordingly. Refrigerate until required.

STEP 2: MUSSEL AND KŪMARA FRITTER BATTER

600 g (1 lb 5 oz) steamed mussels, finely chopped
400 g (14 oz) kūmara, diced into small cubes and cooked
½ cup finely diced red onion
⅓ cup roughly chopped fresh basil
⅓ cup sweet chilli sauce
1 lemon, zest and juice
3 eggs
¾ cup all-purpose flour
flaky sea salt & freshly ground black pepper

Place the chopped mussels, kūmara, red onion, basil, sweet chilli sauce and lemon zest and juice in a bowl. Mix together.

In a separate bowl, place the eggs and flour. With a stick blender, blitz together to make a thick batter.

Fold the batter through the mussel mix, and season with salt and pepper. Refrigerate until required.

STEP 3: COOKING AND SERVING

cooking oil
mussel and kūmara fritter batter
tartare sauce, to serve
lemons, to serve

Preheat the oven to 140°C (275°F).

Place a cast-iron skillet or similar on medium-high heat. Once hot, turn down to medium-low. Add a little oil, then add a tablespoon of the batter to the pan. Cook for 1 to 2 minutes on each side until golden. Cool a little, then taste. Adjust the batter with salt and pepper and lemon juice if needed. If the batter is a little thick and stodgy, thin it with a little milk or water.

Batch-cook the fritters, keeping the cooked fritters warm in the oven until you are finished.

Serve small fritters on a platter with the tartare sauce and lemon wedges on the side. If you have made large fritters, place a couple on each plate, add a liberal dollop of tartare sauce, and finish with a lemon wedge to squeeze over. Eat immediately.

ROASTED FISH BELLY
WITH BRUSCHETTA AND GREEN OR BLACK OLIVE MAYO

The belly is a prized cut from larger fish, like kingfish, bluenose, hāpuka and even larger snapper. I say 'larger', as any of the really large XXL snapper, especially if they are hooked and caught in water that isn't too deep, should be returned to the sea as they are the great breeders. The belly of large tuna are also prized, especially by the Japanese, who often eat it raw as high-grade sashimi. At Depot we often serve kingfish or hāpuka belly when we can get them. They are a firm favourite with the punters.

STEP 1: BRUSCHETTA

1 baguette or ciabatta loaf, or similar
olive oil or cooking oil
flaky sea salt & freshly ground black pepper

Preheat the oven to 180°C (350°C).

Cut the bread in slices up to a centimetre thick. Brush both sides of each slice with oil, place on an oven tray, then season with salt and pepper.

Cook until golden. Check after 5 minutes, then frequently after that. The bruschetta can go from perfect to burnt very quickly. Cool, then store in an airtight container until required.

STEP 2: GREEN OR BLACK OLIVE MAYO

1 cup mayonnaise
⅓ cup green or black olives, pits removed
½ tablespoon lemon juice
flaky sea salt & freshly ground black pepper

Using a stick blender or similar, blitz the mayo with the olives and lemon juice. Taste, then season with salt and pepper. You won't need too much salt, as the olives can be a little salty.

STEP 3: COOKING AND SERVING

fish bellies, skin on, scaled
olive oil
flaky sea salt & freshly ground black pepper
lemons, to serve

Preheat the oven to 180°C (350°F). Place a roasting dish in the oven for 5 to 10 minutes to get searing hot. To a large bowl, add the fish bellies with generous amounts of olive oil and salt and pepper. With clean hands, massage the bellies so they are fully covered in the oil.

Carefully remove the hot roasting dish from the oven. Add a little olive oil, then gently place the bellies skin-side down in the roasting dish.

Place in the oven to cook until golden with some crispy edges. Start checking after 10 minutes. Cooking times will differ depending on the bellies' thickness. Fish bellies have high fat content, so they are very forgiving when cooking.

Serve the bellies either in the roasting pan after it has cooled a little or, using a couple of large spatulas, carefully lift the bellies out and place on a platter. Serve the bruschetta and olive mayo on the side with some lemon halves for squeezing. Eat immediately.

SMOKED KAHAWAI MELT

Kahawai used to be affectionally referred to as the 'people's fish', as you were almost guaranteed to catch a kahawai when you went sea fishing. Alas, not so much these days, and I think we are beginning to understand what a loss that is. Such great scrappers, delicious raw or cooked fresh, and of course they smoke beautifully too. Some fishers say to bleed kahawai, but I'm not in that camp. Bleeding the fish gets rid of some of its blood, but its bloodline remains along the centre of each fillet, and while it's a little stronger in flavour, it's my favourite part. This recipe is super easy and, more importantly, super tasty. You can use any smoked fish you have at hand.

MAKES 12 MELTS

STEP 1: SMOKED KAHAWAI MIX

1 kg (2 lb 4 oz) smoked kahawai
½ cup finely diced red onion
½ cup finely diced gherkin or pickle
2 tablespoons roughly chopped capers
1 cup mayonnaise
½ cup sour cream
1½ tablespoons mustard (use Old Yella Habanero Mustard if it is about)
2 tablespoons lemon juice
flaky sea salt & freshly ground black pepper

In a bowl, with clean hands, roughly break up the smoked kahawai and discard any bones you find. Add all the other ingredients except the salt and pepper. Taste and season accordingly with the salt and pepper. Refrigerate until required.

STEP 2: COOKING AND SERVING

12 slices thick white bread
smoked kahawai mix
grated cheese, such as Edam or Cheddar
lemon wedges, to serve

Turn the oven to the grill setting. Lay out the slices of bread on an oven tray, and place under the grill until golden and crunchy on one side.

Remove the tray, then turn the bread over so the soft, untoasted side is facing up.

Top each slice with liberal amounts of the smoked kahawai mix, then finish with a good layer of the grated cheese.

Place back under the grill. Once the cheese is melted, they are done.

Serve with lemon wedges, and Simply Red Kasundi Ketchup if you have any at hand.

These are so, so good. Go for it!

SPICED FISH WINGS
WITH CORIANDER AND MINT RAITA

Fish wings are actually the throat of fish where it meets the gills. I urge you to use them, as I reckon they're the best part of the fish, but you do need to scale the fish thoroughly. I recommend scaling fish anyway as it makes filleting a far more enjoyable job, and of course cooking fish with skin on is a no brainer. Once you remove the throats, split them down the middle and cut most of the fins off with kitchen shears. While there are bones in the 'wings', they are large and manageable and make eating them fun and super tasty.

STEP 1: CORIANDER AND MINT RAITA

1 cucumber, grated
1 garlic clove, chopped finely
½ cup roughly chopped fresh coriander
½ cup roughly chopped fresh mint
400 g (14 oz) thick, creamy natural yoghurt
1 tablespoon lemon juice
flaky sea salt & freshly ground black pepper

Squeeze out as much juice from the grated cucumber as possible, then place the grated cucumber in a bowl with all the other ingredients except the salt and pepper. Mix to combine, taste and season accordingly with the salt and pepper. Refrigerate until required.

STEP 2: SPICED FISH WINGS

3 tablespoons cumin seeds, roasted and ground
½ tablespoon smoked paprika
3 tablespoons sumac
fresh fish wings
1 lemon, zest and juice
olive oil
flaky sea salt & freshly ground black pepper

Mix the spices together. Place the fish wings in a bowl, and scatter over a liberal amount of the spice. Add the lemon zest and juice, olive oil, salt and pepper. With clean hands, mix it all over and through the wings. Refrigerate until required.

STEP 3: COOKING AND SERVING

cooking oil
marinated fish wings
coriander and mint raita
lemon halves, to serve

Preheat the oven to 200°C (400°F).

Place a roasting dish in the oven for 5 minutes until very hot. Carefully add some cooking oil, then place the wings skin-side down and return to the oven. Cook for 8 to 10 minutes, until the fish pulls away from the bone with no resistance.

Serve on a platter with the raita and lemon halves on the side. Have a roll of paper towels to hand, as you will need them. It's a messy eat but it's fun. You won't believe how good they taste, and I guarantee you'll never discard them from your catch again.

SOUTHERN FRIED BUTTERMILK CRAYFISH TAILS
WITH RANCH DRESSING AND HOT SAUCE

This dish is as decadent as it is down and dirty. It would cost you a large fortune if you splashed out the cash for the crays, so you're more likely to make it if you've found a few 'bugs' in your craypots one morning. You could also make this with bigger-flaked or firmer fillets of fish like hāpuka, bluenose, monkfish or ling. There are a few steps to this recipe but it is definitely worth the effort.

STEP 1: PREPARING CRAYFISH TAIL PIECES

whole live crayfish

Place the crayfish in your freezer for 30 to 40 minutes. This will do two things: put them to sleep (killing them humanely) and make the tail of the crayfish separate from the shell very easily.

Remove the crays from the freezer. Run a sharp knife around the membrane that connects the tail to the head of the crayfish.

Using kitchen scissors, cut down the inside of the tail. Prise open the shell, and remove the tail in one piece. Refrigerate until required.

Use the heads any way you like. I often boil them for a couple of minutes, then remove the legs to eat. I then roast the heads in the oven at 170°C (325°F) for 40 minutes or so, smash them up, place in a saucepan along with roughly chopped onion, celery, carrots and a liberal amount of tomato paste. Cover with water, then simmer away for a few hours to make delicious crayfish stock.

STEP 2: CRAYFISH BUTTERMILK MARINADE

crayfish tails
2 cups buttermilk
1 lemon, zest and juice
1 tablespoon cumin powder
1 tablespoon smoked paprika

Slice the crayfish tails into pieces across the width of the tail. Remember, the pieces will become bigger in size when fried with the coating.

To a bowl, add all the other ingredients. Mix well. Submerge the pieces of crayfish in the buttermilk marinade, and place in the fridge for 1 to 2 hours.

STEP 3: RANCH DRESSING

1 cup mayonnaise
½ cup sour cream
1 tablespoon milk
2 tablespoons cider vinegar
1 teaspoon finely minced garlic
flaky sea salt & freshly ground black pepper

In a bowl, whisk together all the ingredients except the salt and pepper. Taste, then season with salt and pepper. Refrigerate until required.

STEP 4: SPICED FLOUR MIX

2 cups all-purpose flour
1 cup cornflour
3 teaspoons salt
½ tablespoon freshly ground black pepper
1½ tablespoons dried oregano
1 tablespoon mustard powder
1 tablespoon ground cumin
1 tablespoon onion powder
1 tablespoon garlic powder
1 tablespoon ground ginger
2 tablespoons smoked paprika
½ teaspoon cayenne pepper

Place all the ingredients in a bowl and mix thoroughly. Store in an airtight container until required.

STEP 5: COOKING AND SERVING

cooking oil
marinated crayfish pieces
spiced flour mix
ranch dressing
hot sauce
lemons

Preheat the oven to 120°C (235°F) and heat up a deep-fryer to 180°C (350°F). Alternatively, place a cast-iron skillet on high heat with enough oil to shallow-fry. You'll know it's up to temp when you add a small piece of bread and it turns golden and crunchy in about a minute.

Dip the crayfish pieces into the spiced flour mix. Rest for 1 to 2 minutes to help the spiced flour mix stick to the crayfish.

Batch-cook the pieces for 2 to 3 minutes until golden and cooked through. Keep warm in the oven while cooking the remaining pieces.

Serve with the ranch dressing on the side for dipping, along with hot sauce and lemon halves. Eat up!

INDEX

B
backing 34
Bacon Chowder, Fish Head and 128–29
bag limit 34
bail 34
bait 34 *see also* burley
barb 34
barbless hooks 35, 54–55
Best Fish Pie Ever 126–27
bird's nest 35
blind casting 35
blood and guts 35
boat fishing 88–91
boat speak 90
boil-up 35
brackish water 35
braid 35
breaking strain 35
Bruschetta 134
burley 35, 95–96 *see also* chum

C
cast 35, 102–3 *see also* surfcasting
catch and release 24–25, 35
Chocolate Fish Slice, Lucky 130
Chocolate Icing 130
Chowder, Fish Head and Bacon 128–29
chum 36
cooking 121–39
Coriander and Mint Raita 137
Crayfish Tails, Southern Fried Buttermilk 138–39

D
'Depot' Fish Sliders 125
drag 36
Dressing, Ranch 139
drift fishing 36
drogue 36
drop-off 36

E
eddy 36

F
filleting 31, 114–17
Fish Belly, Roasted 134–35
Fish Head and Bacon Chowder 128–29
Fish Head Stock 128
fish on 36
Fish Pie Ever, Best 126–27
Fish Sliders, 'Depot' 125
Fish Wings, Spiced 137
flasher rigs 36
floatant 107
floating lines 104–105
fluorocarbon 36
fly box 107, 108
fly fishing 100–109
  casting 102–103
  dry dropper 102
  dry fly 102, 108
  gear 104–109
  nymph 102, 108
  wet fly / streamer 102, 108
forceps 107
foul 36
foul-hooked 36
free spool 36
Fritters, Mussel and Kūmara 132–33

G
gear *see* kit
gimbal belt 36

H
harling 37
hats 42–43
  baseball caps 42
  beanies 43
  Brixton Fiddler caps 43
  bucket 42
  fedora 43
  Foreign Legion caps 43
  newsboy flat caps 43
  trucker caps 42
hooks 37, 54–55
  barbless 35, 54–55
  circle 54
  double 55
  'J' 55
  treble 55

I
Icing, Chocolate 130
iki 113
indicators 107

J
jig 37

K
Kahawai Melt, Smoked 136
kayak fishing *see* boat fishing
kit *see also* hooks, lures, reels, rigs, rods, sinkers
  for boat fishing 91
  for fly fishing 109
  for surfcasting 97
  for wharf fishing 85
knots 70–75
  blood 72
  double uni 75
  half blood 73
  improved clinch 74
  leader 37
  lefty's loop 75
  surgeon's loop 74
Kūmara Fritters, Mussel and 132–33

L
leader knot 37
leaders 37, 105
Lemon Mayo, Preserved 125
let it run 37
lines 104–5
  braid 35
  floating 104–5
  fluorocarbon 36
  monofilament 37
  shooting head 105
  sinking 105
lingo 20, 34–39, 90

Lucky Chocolate Fish Slice 130
lures 37, 56–61 *see also* jig
   gamefish 56
   inchiku jigs 60
   micro jigs 60
   poppers 58–59
   sliding-head 59–60
   slow-pitch jigs 59
   soft baits 56–58
   speed jigs 61
   spinners 59
   squid jigs 61
   stick baits 58

M
mainline 37
Māori fishing 18–21
   early practices 18–20
   legends 21
   terms 20
Māori legends 21
   Māui and the giant fish 21
   Tangaroa and Ikatere 21
match the hatch 37
Mayo, Green or Black Olive 134
Mayo, Preserved Lemon 125
Melt, Smoked Kahawai 136
monofilament 37
Mussel and Kūmara Fritters 132–33

N
nets 107

O
off the bricks 37
Olive Mayo, Green or Black 134
outrigger 37
oxbow 37

P
parts of fish 30–31
Pie Ever, Best Fish 126–27
pillies 37
Preserved Lemon Mayo 125

R
Raita, Coriander and Mint 137
Ranch Dressing 139

recipes 125–39
reels 37, 50–53
   baitcasting 53
   fly 104
   game-fishing 53
   overhead 51
   soft-bait 53
   spinning 51
   surfcasting 53
retrieve 38
rigs 38, 64–67
   deepwater live bait 65
   dropper 65
   ledger 65
   running 65
   sabiki 66
   top water live bait with balloon 66
Roasted Fish Belly 134–35
rod action 38
rods 38, 46–49, 104
   boat 47
   fly-fishing 49
   jig 49
   soft-bait 48
   surfcasting 47
   telescopic 48–49
   top water 48
   travelling 48–49
   ultra-light fishing 48

S
safety 78–79, 97
saltwater fishing rigs *see* rigs
Sashimi 131
scaling 114
scissors 107
set the hook 38
shooting heads 105
sinkers 38, 62–63
   ball 63
   breakaway 63
   clip-on 63
   egg 63
   fixed 62
   split-shot 63
   stationary 62
sinking lines 105
skirt 38

skunked 38
Slice, Lucky Chocolate Fish 130
Sliders, 'Depot' Fish 125
Smoked Kahawai Melt 136
snips 107
Southern Fried Buttermilk Crayfish Tails 138–39
species of fish 27–29
Spiced Fish Wings 137
spooked 38
spool 38
Stock, Fish Head 128
straylining 38
strike 38
surfcasting 94–97
sustainability 24–31
   catch and release 24–25, 35
   catching a range of species 27–29
   using all of the fish 30–31
swivel 38

T
tackle 38
Tartare Sauce 132
terminal tackle 39
terms *see* lingo
tight lines! 39
tippets 39, 105
top water 39
trace *see* leaders
trolling 39
turn up your drag 39
types of fishing 82–109
   fly fishing 100–109
   small boat or kayak fishing 88–91
   surfcasting 94–97
   wharf fishing 82–85

W
waders 107–8
wharf fishing 82–85
whopper stopper 39
wind knot 39

ABOUT THE AUTHOR

Al Brown is a chef, TV presenter and writer. He runs Depot Oyster Bar & Eatery, Federal Delicatessen and Best Ugly Bagels. He has written several bestselling cookbooks, including *Go Fish*, *Stoked* and *Eat Up New Zealand: The Bach Edition*.

Al's love of fishing began at an early age and, now he is older, nothing has really changed. He still gets a kick out of any fishing mission, be it on the ocean, walking up a river or casting from the shore.